Female Dog Names

A Complete Guide to Help You Name Your Cute Girl Puppy

Bonus chapter and free resource guide available at **www.thedogtrainingplanet.com/bonus**

Disclaimer and legal notice

Contents

Introduction

Baby naming has become somewhat of a sport in the modern world we live in. There is certainly a competitive edge to the whole thing, with soon-to-be parents (or even just couples who think that babies may be on the horizon) "claiming" names or remaining incredibly secretive about their choices until their child is born, for fear that someone might try to steal their name. Celebrities are becoming known for their over the top attempts to out-do the last with the most unique name of the century, and everyone else is following suit – searching for the name that will set them and their child apart.

This seems to be a fairly new phenomenon, as parents shy away from names that could be considered common or popular. They are opting instead for unique spellings of traditional names, or names that were invented entirely for the purpose of ensuring their child would never have to face the shame of sharing a name with another child in their classroom.

Because somewhere along the way, being one of 12 Jennifers apparently became shameful.

What's interesting is that this is a trend that has always taken place in the doggy naming world. Not the competitiveness or the desire to pick a name solely to set your dog apart, but certainly the drive towards distinctive. Think about it. The names of your friend's pets growing up were probably names you never would have thought of yourself. They were unique and personal to the pet owners, names chosen with love and care, and without a lot of concern for what others outside the family might think of a particular moniker.

And isn't that how it should be? Getting a puppy is a very special event in most people's lives. There is a reason they say dogs are man's best friend – because adding a canine to your life means committing the next 10 to 15 years to this loyal companion who will love and cherish you just as much as you do her. And while your commitment to a puppy won't last as long as, say, your commitment to a baby, that doesn't mean the love you feel for your pup is any less valuable.

Or that the sacred tradition of naming should be any less worthy of thought and contemplation.

In fact, plenty of people think of their pups as children, and they love and care for them as such. It isn't uncommon at all to hear women talking about their "fur babies" or to see couples and families always opting to include their pets in their Christmas photos. Because even if you wouldn't go so far as to call your new puppy your baby, she is still certainly a part of your family. And there is no denying the depths of your love for her.

Our dogs have a fascinating way of quickly integrating themselves into our lives and becoming indispensible to us – the companions we love and rely on. And that level of importance means they are worthy of a name chosen with just as much love and care as any baby name.

This is why I have put together this book meant to guide you through the process of naming your puppy; an important decision that deserves your thought and effort. After all, this is a name you will be shouting from your back porch and around your house for years to come. It is the name you will be introducing your puppy as to strangers on the street and the one you will always remember as being representative of your loyal and trusted friend.

Still, as personal a decision as naming your pup can be, plenty of people find themselves stumped when they first hold that precious ball of fur in their arms. Maybe it's the puppy breath and the sweet puppy kisses that disorients us, but every name you had in your head before, might just go out the window as soon as you find yourself looking into those eyes; suddenly feeling as though nothing fits quite right.

Don't worry; you aren't alone in your loss for a name. This is a phenomenon that affects many a new puppy owner, and it is one that is easily resolved. First, don't put too much pressure on yourself – you don't have to pick out a name overnight. Your new puppy will still be acclimating to her surroundings while you try to figure out the perfect name for her, and spending a few days getting to know her personality can actually help.

But we'll get to that. In the pages ahead, I'm going to guide you through the various inspirations for puppy names. My goal is to help you decide what kind of name will fit your puppy best, and how to choose a name from there. Then, the final chapter of this book will introduce you to the Top 500 Female Dog Names. Maybe you want to select one straight from the list, or perhaps you want to veer off towards even more creative options. Either way, those names should be a great jumping off point for you to select the name that perfectly fits this new puppy you already love and adore.

3

By the time we're through, I have no doubt you'll know exactly what name it is your puppy was always meant to be called.

After that, I want to encourage you to check out a bonus chapter, free on my website:

www.thedogtrainingplanet.com/bonus

Titled: *Now That You've Got Your Name: 5 Things You Absolutely Must Know About Owning a New Puppy*, this bonus chapter is going to walk you through all the other important bits of information you will need as a new dog owner.

In addition, you can also download there a resource guide with useful dog training tools – "My Everyday Dog Training Tools – Free Resource Guide".

Together they have important tips and hints about training and what you can expect now that you are a new puppy owner – a jumping off point for the next several years of your life.

So let's get started. That sweet girl of yours needs a name, and you need to know what to call her. Because "Puppy" won't work as a name forever.

Or would it?

Chapter 1: Congratulations on Your New Pet

She's here. The puppy you have been waiting for forever, or the one who caught you by surprise and was just too sweet *not* to adopt. However long or short your decision making period in getting a puppy, she's here now. And you couldn't be more in love.

So first things first, congratulations. You have just made one of the best decisions of your life, and this sweet girl is sure to become a cherished member of your family and world. Just looking into her eyes now, you already know that to be true. She has captured your heart and won you over completely.

It's amazing how much we can love a little 4-legged ball of fur, isn't it?

People go to varying levels of effort when it comes to bringing a puppy into their life. Some spend weeks and months researching, seeking out the perfect breed to suit their needs and then vetting breeders to find one that operates in a humane and responsible ways. It isn't uncommon for these people to find a puppy located states away that they have to then transport to them, resulting in a moment of love and affection that is too sweet to miss when puppy and owner are finally introduced.

For others, adopting a puppy isn't so much about choosing the right breed as it is about providing a home for a pup that otherwise might not have one. People seem to think that only adult dogs are available for adoption, but most shelters will tell you that there are times when puppies come through their doors looking for homes, as well. Often these are mixed-breed pets where the origin of both parents isn't always known. You won't likely get papers on these dogs or make any kind of money off their offspring, but that isn't why you decided to get a puppy in the first place, is it? You just knew, as soon as you looked into that little one's eyes, that she was meant to be yours.

And you hers.

However your puppy came into your life, she's here now and the two of you have most of the next two decades to make memories and fall even further in love.

What an exciting time.

To get started though, there are a few priorities actually more important than giving her a name. Things like:

- Getting her Food
- Deciding Where She Will Sleep
- Making Sure She's Healthy

Food

Most puppy necessities aren't really necessities. You can go a few days before worrying about getting her toys or treats. Even a doggy bed doesn't have to happen overnight, depending on where you want her to sleep. But food? That's a priority.

Just like babies, puppies are working on growing up big and strong. Even the tiniest of breeds still have some growing to do from puppyhood. Most puppies are still growing until they are 12 to 18 months old, and eating is a big part of ensuring they grow up healthy.

So how often should you be feeding your puppy? Well, talk to your veterinarian about breed specifics, but most pups should be eating three to four times a day. With puppies, you don't necessarily want to just dump all their food in a bowl and count on them to regulate their intake throughout the day. They aren't always prepared for such a big responsibility, and may eat too much at once, causing stomachaches and digestion issues.

Smaller meals are easier for pups to digest, and spacing their feedings out can ensure their energy levels remain consistent throughout the day.

As for what kind of puppy food to pick up, that's another question to talk to your vet about. But while waiting for an appointment, stick to puppy specific brands. Just like formula for a baby, these brands are specially designed for the needs of your growing pup. They often include extra vitamins and nutrients, and they are formulated to accommodate a puppy's more sensitive digestive system.

Sleep

Figuring out where your puppy is going to sleep is actually a more important decision than you might think. Some people are perfectly fine with sharing their bed with their dog. In fact, it's the option they would most prefer. They love having an extra body to snuggle with at night. But for other people, keeping the pups out of the bed is important. Which means having an alternate plan in place and utilizing it from the start.

Because once you let your puppy sleep in your bed, she's going to decide that is always where she was meant to be – and breaking the habit can be tough.

So if you have other plans for where your pup is going to sleep, perhaps in a crate or a dog bed in the living room, the sooner you set that situation up and start creating a routine, the better.

Health

No matter where you got your puppy from, getting her in for a checkup and her first round of shots from the vet as soon as possible is important. If you have adopted from the pound, they may have already taken care of some of that for you, but even still – getting her in to see your vet can provide the peace of mind that all is well.

Questions to ask your vet during that appointment might include:

- What brand of food is best for my puppy?
- What shot schedule will she need to be on?
- When should I have my puppy spayed?
- Should I get her tattooed or microchipped, in case she gets lost?
- Are there specifics about my puppy's breed that are important for me to know?
- What kind of treats can I give my puppy?
- Is there a good dog park in the area I can take her to?
- How often should I bring her into the vet?
- What is the after hours policy here, in case there is an emergency?

- Are there any books on training my puppy that you would recommend?

You have plenty of time to come up with a name, but dealing with the food, sleep and health issues should be a priority in your first few days with your new pup. The good news is that also provides you the time you need to get to know your girl and her personality. And the more you know about her, the better prepared you will be to pick a name that suits her perfectly.

In the meantime, enjoy these special days of bonding with your new companion. She is going to come to realize that you are the one providing comfort and food to her, and with that will come a loyalty that surpasses any you could find in the human world. So enjoy the extra snuggles in these first few days where she may be more skittish and unsure. Remember that she is in an entirely new place and will likely need a little more reassurance and love from you.

Just like a newborn, now is the time to provide her with the care and connection to make her feel safe and secure in her surroundings. Once she does, she will begin to show you facets of her personality that may just lead you to the perfect name.

What a fun time you two are about to have together.

Chapter 2: What's in a Name? The Importance of Choosing the Right Name For Your New Girl

"A rose by any other name would smell as sweet." They are the words uttered by Juliet in Shakespeare's play, *Romeo and Juliet*. She speaks them in an attempt to argue that the names Montague and Capulet mean nothing – that those names alone certainly shouldn't be what keep the two lovers apart.

In that context, it's hard not to agree with Juliet. She's a young girl in love, searching for reasons to hold on to that love and fight against the forces that would keep them apart. Even more importantly, her argument is sound. After all, our names aren't really something most of us get a say in. Certainly, they become a part of our identity, but do they define us?

Should they?

Juliet had a point. But when you start to ask what's in a name, you also run the risk of minimizing the importance of our monikers. No, they don't define us. But that doesn't mean they don't still hold value, both for our four-legged friends and for us.

You probably identify with your name more than you know. And all of us have known someone at some point in our lives who gave a name certain associations, as well. Whether we mean for it to happen or not, names carry a weight to them. They hold value, both good and bad.

Because of that, what you name your dog matters. Not because you should care what other people think about that name, but because it is a name you are going to be saying for a long time to come. It is a name that will become a part of your dog's identity, and a part of your family narrative. You want it to be the right name. One that fits and flows naturally when talking to and about your dog.

The name matters. And while it isn't a life or death decision, it is one that carries an importance worthy of the time and effort you are putting into this choice.

So congratulations to you for recognizing that while a rose by any other name would still smell sweet, it just wouldn't be the same if it were called a "booger" instead.

Still, before you put too much thought into your decision, you're probably wondering just how important this really is. In fact, you may be wondering what's to stop you from flipping to the end of this book, closing your eyes, and picking a name at random – just to get this whole naming business over with.

Well, not only does your sweet girl deserve more thought than that, but there are a few things to consider when it comes to the importance of a name.

A Name You Like

You are probably going to be saying this name several times a day for the next 10 to 15 years of your life. You will probably wind up saying it far more than you even say your own name. Which means, you want to pick a name you actually like. One you don't mind saying and that won't annoy you over time.

11

You would be surprised how common it is to actually pick a name you eventually come to hate. Or how many dog owners give their kids naming privileges, only to wind up with a dog name that is so ridiculous and over the top, they find themselves avoiding saying it whenever possible.

Nobody wants to find him or herself in that position. This is the newest member of your family. She is someone who is going to be by your side for years to come. You want to love her name as much as you love her. Which is why picking a name on the fly isn't an advisable way to go for anyone. Just like a tattoo, the permanence of this decision is long lasting. The name you pick is the one you will be stuck with. You don't want to leave a decision like that to chance.

Short and Sweet

There are so many funny dog names that include several different names in one. In fact, in a later chapter we will be discussing how adding a title to a name (such as Miss or Lady) can make that name all the more humorous. But if you name your puppy The Duchess of Bubbles and Lace, you are going to realize very quickly that you have gone too far.

Yes, it is a funny name. But imagine trying to call out that name every morning as you alert your puppy to her bowl being filled.

"Duchess of Bubbles and Lace, come here."

"No, Duchess of Bubbles and Lace. Don't pee in the corner."

"Who wants a treat? Does Duchess of Bubbles and Lace want a treat?"

You see what I'm getting at here, right? If you give your puppy a name that is too long, you will grow to regret it very quickly. Don't pick a name that is a mouthful, unless you plan on shortening it from the beginning. And even then, ask yourself how important it really is to have such a long moniker in place if you are just going to give her a nickname anyway.

A Name That Fits

Let's say you named your puppy before you ever even met her. Maybe you decided that you always wanted a puppy named Frisky, and so you anointed your pup with that one right away. Only, as the days and weeks go on, you come to realize that your puppy is one of the mellowest girls you have ever met. She seems to prefer to spend all her time in your lap, and doesn't even show much interest in taking walks. In fact, she is a bit skittish around other people and tends to cower behind you whenever confronted by strangers or other dogs.

Suddenly, Frisky seems like a silly name for her, doesn't it?

There is something to be said for irony in a name, and we'll be discussing that later as well. But naming a dog Frisky who is anything but, might just get awkward for all involved. And trust me when I say that you will soon grow tired of people joking about how ill fitting her name truly is.

Not all names have personality connotations, but there are certainly plenty of names that wouldn't seem fitting for all dogs. Have you ever met a grown adult who has a name that doesn't seem to suit her? Perhaps she goes by a nickname instead, or maybe she has even opted to legally change her name – just because she so loathes the one she was given at birth. If this can happen to people, you had better believe it is possible to give your dog the wrong name as well.

You don't want to name her something that doesn't fit her or her personality. Remember, she's going to spend the rest of her life with this name, and so are you. You want it to be the right name; the one that will always seem like it was meant just for her.

Training Conflicts

Not every dog owner plans on going all out with training, but for those who do — considering training commands prior to choosing a name can be important.

Dogs are intelligent, but they are limited in their understanding of our spoken language. They tend to rely on sounds more than anything when trying to interpret what you are communicating. As such, they may not always recognize the difference between two similarly sounding words. Which is why you don't want to give your dog a name that could conflict with commands you would otherwise use.

For instance, if you plan on teaching your dog to "sit", you probably don't want to name her Spit. Or if "heel" is a command you intend to give, Beale might be a name you want to avoid.

Again, this won't be something that applies to everyone, but it is worth thinking about. You can always alter your commands later on if you come to realize there is a conflict with the name you chose, but the most common commands are going to be the ones used by others as well. Which means you'll also have to consider how your puppy may respond to commands she hears in the dog park that otherwise sound very similar to her name.

You don't want her running off in the other direction every time another dog owner calls out for his or her puppy to stay.

A Name All Her Own

Sure, plenty of families have members of the same name. It isn't uncommon at all for a Junior to be born into a family and for father and son to embrace having the same name. There may be some instances of confusion over time, but for the most part — all involved figure out how to differentiate between Senior and Junior easily enough.

Unfortunately, dogs don't have the same level of understanding when it comes to sharing a name. In fact, if you give a dog a name that is shared by your daughter or best friend, anyone she is likely to be around regularly, you are asking for a world of confusion every time that name is muttered.

Think about it. Puppies grow to recognize their names as being indicative of good or exciting interactions to come. We say their name with a smile on our face, ready to welcome their kisses and cuddles. We beckon them to us by calling that name when we want to take them for a walk or give them a treat. At mealtimes, we call out their names to let them know food is being served. That name is theirs, and it becomes associated with the pleasant feelings of being wanted and loved.

So if you also use that name in association with someone else with regularity, there is bound to be confusion. And if your puppy grows used to hearing her name, without those good connotations that would otherwise accompany it, it's possible she may never learn her name at all.

Which is why you also want to be careful of names that even just sound like those you might otherwise utter in your house. You want your puppy to recognize her name and to know it as her own. So making it a name that truly is all her own is important.

No Shame

Finally, you want a name that you can shout at the dog park without shame or embarrassment. You may have laughed right along with your kids when they suggested the name "Sugar Bottom Bum Drop", but are you still going to be laughing when you have to yell it from your front porch at night as your neighbors look on?

Levels of embarrassment vary for everyone, and you may have just such a sense of humor that calling out Sugar Bottom Bum Drop in public wouldn't embarrass you at all. But what about a name that

15

has negative connotations or could be taken offensively by others? Anything that might be mistaken as a racial slur or some kind of threat should also be avoided. You don't want your puppy's name to ever become a point of contention.

Don't make the mistake of picking a name without thought that you will eventually come to regret or be embarrassed about. If doing so is something you want to avoid, it might be a good idea to run any names you come up with by friends and family, just to make sure there isn't anything potentially embarrassing or offensive that you are missing. Running the name through Urban Dictionary is also always a good idea, as various slang words are coming into popularity all the time and the name you are thinking of could have connotations you never even knew about. You wouldn't want the seemingly innocuous name you chose to wind up being something your high school niece and nephew snicker at every time they hear it.

Obviously, with an ever-evolving language, there are some things that may be impossible to avoid. But if you put some care into your naming decision, you should come out in the end with a name you will never be embarrassed to call for.

A Rose By Any Other Name

So you see, there is a lot more to a name than Juliet was originally trying to argue. And putting this level of thought into what you name your puppy is exactly what you *should* be doing. You wouldn't name your child by closing your eyes and picking a random name off a list, and you shouldn't employ that method for naming your puppy either.

The name matters, both to you and your little girl. It will communicate a lot about the both of you to others, and it will be a name that will become as common for you to utter as your own. Which is why you want it to be the right name. You want it to be the "rose" that perfectly fits this puppy you already love so much.

The name you would never even think to question as the years go by.

Because it is just so perfect, there is no denying it was always meant to be the name for your sweet girl.

Chapter 3: What Might Influence Your Naming Decision?

There are so many questions to ask yourself when it comes to getting a puppy.

- Do you care about breeds? And if so, do you care enough to want a purebred puppy? Also, how much research have you put into your chosen breed? Are you sure they will be compatible with you, your home and your lifestyle?
- When it comes to size, are you hoping for a small, medium or large dog? Can your home and lifestyle accommodate the various challenges and needs of dogs of each size?
- Are you adopting from a shelter? If so, will shots be taken care of before or after the adoption is complete?
- Or are you committed to seeking out an ethical breeder? And what questions are you asking to ensure the breeder you choose is, in fact, ethical?

- What kind of activities do you want your puppy for? Are you hoping for a running partner or a typical lap dog?
- Will you find your puppy locally, or have to arrange travel from out of state? If you have to arrange travel, are you prepared for the extra costs associated with that?
- Do you have children, and have you therefore researched breeds that are good with kids?
- What about shedding, barking, digging and other behaviors common to specific breeds – do you want to avoid them, or do you not really have a preference?
- Do you want her to be an indoor or outdoor pet?

Like I said, there are so many questions to consider, not the least of which being what you will name your puppy when you finally have her. And just as your answers to each of the questions above will be unique to you and your situation, so will your influences when it comes to naming your pup.

That's the beautiful thing about the human condition. We all have a different take on the world as we experience it, and those differences alter how we process information around us and the decisions we ultimately make. Whether you realize it or not, there are external forces influencing you in unique and personal ways all the time. And those influences will play a large role in the name you decide to give your pup in the end.

Don't believe me? Well, let's explore some of the influences that may have some pull on the name you eventually select – then you can decide for yourself how strong those influences actually are in your life and situation.

Personality Traits

We have already discussed this to some extent, but your puppy's personality will absolutely play a role in the name you select. You very well may meet her and realize that the name you had in mind previously just isn't a great fit after all. Or, alternately, you could meet her and realize that her personality just begs for her to have a name you otherwise hadn't even considered.

Dogs are as individualistic as we are, and treating them as such is important.

If you've ever named a baby, you know there are a lot of factors to consider. There are names that seem great for children, but are not necessarily suited for adults – and vice versa. Then there are names that conjure up certain images and seem to reflect certain traits, even when those traits aren't expressly indicated by the name itself. When you hear the name Jessica, for instance, you might automatically flash back to the captain of your high school cheer squad. The name itself could leave you thinking of a bright and bubbly personality, one that wouldn't necessarily fit the introverted bookworm in the corner of the library.

These associations are obviously personal, and don't apply to everyone. A lot of them have to do with our unique experiences and the people we have known in our lives, although it is difficult to argue that some names do have connotations that seem to be somewhat universal – as evidenced by Hollywood's inclination towards certain names for specific character types.

All that to say, if you take the time to get to know your puppy's personality, it will undoubtedly influence your naming decision. This is just a matter of whether or not you choose to name her right away, or wait a few days before selecting a moniker. The longer you wait, though, the more likely her personality is going to be a influencing factor on your decision. We just can't help but make those associations – which is exactly why you should wait to take her personality into account before selecting a name. Because if you don't, and you wind up choosing a name that doesn't actually fit her, you will likely grow to regret that name with time.

Celebrity Influences

Whether we like it or not, celebrities have a lot of pull on the decisions we make and how we live our lives. Sure, we may make fun of them or cringe at their bad behavior, but we are always watching them – even if we don't realize it.

When you check out at the grocery store, you are accosted by magazines telling you everything that is happening in the lives of the rich and famous. Even if you don't pick those magazines up, you see them. You find out who is getting divorced, who is pregnant and who is kissing whom in those split second updates captioned across the magazine covers. This information is practically spoon fed to us in such a way that we can't help but take it in.

If you ever turn on your television, you are inundated with even more celebrity gossip. We are a culture that is obsessed with our celebrities, and everything they do – from what they have for breakfast to how they style their hair – becomes fodder for our ever-curious minds. Even if it doesn't seem interesting or entertaining to you, there is no avoiding this dump of information that is continuously updating us on the lives of those in the spotlight.

Which means that those celebrities can influence both your baby naming and puppy naming decisions. Even if you don't realize it or never set out to let a celebrity influence you in the first place.

Let's say you're standing in line at the store and you absentmindedly catch the name of the latest celebrity baby. You don't think much of it, but that name winds up rolling around in your head. It digs in and becomes a point of reference as either a name you do or do not like.

Months later, when it comes time to name your puppy, that name may pop into your head seemingly out of the blue. You probably won't even remember where you heard it, at least not until you start telling people your puppy's name and they reply with, "Oh, you mean like Reese Witherspoon's little girl?"

And then, it hits you – you totally named your dog after a celebrity baby.

Sometimes, the influence is far more intentional than that. Maybe you just like the name, or perhaps you are being ironic. You could name your pup Apple in an attempt to poke fun at Gwyneth Paltrow, or you may be one of the many dog owners who intentionally names his or her new puppy after a favorite celebrity outright. Making clear the overt influence celebrities truly do have over these choices.

Physical Characteristics

Just as personality can play an important role in your naming decision, the influence of physical characteristics also shouldn't be discounted.

Plenty of pet owners choose names based in part, or entirely, on their dog's looks. Pups that are going to grow to be especially big or petite are routinely subjected to this, as are those with unique markings or distinguishable fur characteristics.

Often, pet owners will even opt for irony in relation to physical traits. They may name their Great Dane "Tiny", for instance, or their Chihuahua "Beast". Even though the names themselves are not a direct reflection of the physical characteristics actually carried by their dog, they are a play on those characteristics and a humorous way of acknowledging the extremes.

If you go through the list of names friends and family have chosen for their own pets, you will likely find that physical characteristics play at least a small part in the names selected more often than not. Even more importantly, you will again find that this wasn't necessarily always intentional. There are just some names we automatically associate with certain physical traits, even when the name itself doesn't outright indicate that trait. Your smaller pup, for instance, is probably going to call for a more delicate name than your larger breed pup – a distinction you may make without even realizing why.

Have no doubt, though, that what she looks like will certainly play a role in the name you eventually choose.

Giving the Kiddos a Say

If you have kids yourself, rest assured, they are going to want a say in the naming of your new pup. Whether this is the first family dog, or she will be joining a few older doggy friends, your kids are going to be ecstatic to welcome the newest member of your family. And that excitement is going to translate into wanting to stake their claim – which for a lot of kids, means being the one to choose a name. Be prepared for that, especially, if you have more than one child. This could easily become a competition, and the kind of thing you will need to referee in order to avoid fights over the new puppy's name.

Even if you don't have kids of your own, though, any of the children in your life will likely have opinions on what you should name your new pup. From nieces and nephews to neighbors and students, kids take pet naming pretty seriously. And they are all going to think they have just the name for you.

Some of these names are going to be ridiculous, the kind of thing that you would never actually want to name a pet. But even then, you will have to tread carefully – not wanting to hurt anyone's feelings by outright laughing at a name they are taking very seriously. So always tell the little ones in your life that you will add their name "to the list" and let them know how much you appreciate their creativity.

What will surprise you even more, however, will be the names these kiddos in your life come up with that actually seem like valid possibilities. Kids are more tuned in to this kind of thing than you might realize, and it is more than possible that one of the children in your life will come up with the perfect name – or at least a name that inspires the perfect name. They are unencumbered by the fear of looking silly that inhibits some of the rest of us, and they really do have a level of creativity that is unparalleled by most adults. So don't plan on automatically discounting the names suggested by the little ones in your life.

You may find that they prove to be a greater influence then you originally would have given them credit for.

Breed Influences

Finally, don't be surprised if your pup's breed comes into play when you set about selecting a name. Often, a puppy's origin can actually prove to be quite beneficial when choosing the unique moniker you are searching for.

For instance, you might find yourself leaning towards a name that rhymes with the breed name or shares characteristics of that name, just for fun or because it actually seems to work. Oodles the Poodle could be a perfect example of this, or Pom-Pom the Pomeranian.

Then there are the names that just seem to go hand in hand with certain breeds, mostly because of the famous dogs we all already know and love of that breed. Anytime you see a Collie, you probably automatically think of the name Lassie, and seeing a Cocker Spaniel may lead you back to the name Lady (from Lady and the Tramp) each and every time. These famous dogs have made an indelible mark on their breed, and you may find yourself leaning towards one of those names for your pet of the same breed, simply because it feels so familiar.

Finally, foreign breeds open themselves up perfectly for a name with a foreign influence. Plenty of people opt for Spanish names for their Chihuahuas, and there are a lot of German options for your German shepherd as well. You certainly don't have to be tied into a foreign name simply because you have a pup of foreign descent, but it opens up possibilities you may not have otherwise thought of;

either because you truly want to honor your puppy's heritage, or because you simply think that doing so is humorous. One way or another, though, that heritage may have more of an influence than you would have originally thought.

The Choice is Still Yours

After all that, you may be feeling a bit overwhelmed by all the influences you didn't even realize were affecting this decision. The reality is, this is true of each and every decision we ever make. There are always outside forces exerting their influence, with or without our being cognizant of that sway. This isn't something to fight against, it just… is. Every choice we make is influenced by something.

But that doesn't mean the ultimate choice isn't still yours to make. Yes, it will probably be influenced by one (or several) of the factors mentioned already. And there may even be other factors at play that we haven't discussed here. But whatever you eventually decide to call your pup, it will have been your name – the one you chose. And you can make that name as unique or generic as you please. You can also choose to rely on whatever influences seem the most on-point to you.

In the end, the only opinions that truly matter are those of you and your family. You are the ones who will be repeating this name again and again over the years, so finding a name you all feel comfortable with should be the main priority, no matter what factors might influence that name.

Besides, no one else ever has to know what your real influences were. Just embrace the name you love, and go with it.

Chapter 4: Famous Dog Names and What Celebrities are Naming Their Pets

Speaking of inspiration, let's get back to some of the famous names that may inspire you in your quest to find the perfect moniker for your sweet little girl.

Yes, there is something to be said for having a unique name. But the truth is that there are so many options to choose from when it comes to naming your pet, even if you pick a more popular name – you aren't likely going to come across many other dogs in real life with the same name. That's because, as we have already discussed, people all have different influences on the choices they make here. And unlike names for babies, there are far less social restrictions on what you name your dog. So realistically, no matter what you choose, it is going to be unique in your little corner of the world.

Which means the sky really is the limit when it comes to picking out that perfect name.

So don't be ashamed of perusing lists of famous dog names, or names that celebrities are giving to their own pets, in your search for inspiration. You may find that one of those names just feels right for your little girl, or that it influences you in the direction of the name that you *will* ultimately choose.

Sure, it may be a name shared by a more famous canine. Or one that has been splashed across movie credits for a decade now. But your puppy doesn't have to know that.

Famous Dogs

Why don't we start with famous dog names. These are the dogs that have made you laugh and cry with their stories of heroics and loyalty. Some of them are real life pets that have done amazing things; so amazing that they have captured the hearts of people worldwide and found themselves as front news stories. While others are fictionalized dogs that have come to feel incredibly real to you over the years through novels and screen adaptations.

A lot of these dogs have become so engrained in our popular culture that their names just feel like natural extensions of their breed. You may find this has already been true of your pup, with your natural inclination being to name her after a famous dog of the

27

same breed. Don't necessarily shy away from that inclination too quickly — it's normal to have that pull, and you may find that the name really is the best fit for your girl.

The good news is, if you opt to go in the direction of a famous dog name — people will routinely pick up on the connection, and it can be a fun icebreaker with introductions and meetings at the dog park.

So who are some of the most famous canines to date? Well, why don't you test yourself by seeing how many of these you already know.

- **Argos:** Odysseus's faithful dog mentioned in Homer's *Odyssey*, who recognizes him after his twenty year absence returning from the Siege of Troy.
- **Backup:** A young private investigator's loyal sidekick in the show *Veronica Mars*.
- **Beethoven:** The lovable St. Bernard featured in a series of children's movies of the same name.
- **Benji:** A fictionalized mixed breed dog that is adopted by a nice family in his own movie.
- **Blue:** A cartoon dog of the popular show *Blue's Clues*.
- **Bo:** President Obama's Portuguese Water Dog, who was gifted to his daughters after the grueling 2008 election period was over.
- **Bobby:** The 19th century Skye Terrier (now known as Greyfriars Bobby) who spent 14 years at his owner's grave in Edinburgh. There is even a statue of him there, and several books and films have been based on his life.
- **Bruiser:** The Chihuahua loved by Elle Woods in the *Legally Blonde* movies.
- **Captain:** A real life German Shepherd who has become known for returning to the gravesite of his deceased owner every night since the man died in 2006.

- **Clifford:** A fictionalized "Big Red Dog" who is popular in children's books and movies.
- **Comet:** The beloved Golden Retriever on *Full House*.
- **Cujo:** A 200-pound Saint Bernard who found fame in the Stephen King novel that shared his name.
- **Fluffy:** The fictionalized supernatural dog featured in *Harry Potter and the Sorcerer's Stone*.
- **Hercules:** The large English Mastiff who terrorizes the neighborhood boys in the 1993 movie *The Sandlot*.
- **Hooch:** A French Mastiff who teamed up with Tom Hanks in *Turner & Hooch* as part of a hilarious police duo.
- **Lassie:** The fictionalized Collie who became America's favorite dog starting in 1943, most famously saving little Timmy from the well.
- **Lex:** A German Shepherd active-duty military dog who is most well known for refusing to leave the side of her handler, who was killed in the line of duty.
- **Marley:** The mischievous Labrador Retriever featured in the *Marley and Me* book and movie.
- **Millie:** Former president George Bush's English Springer Spaniel, who was so popular that she "wrote" a book, which became a number one *New York Times* best seller.
- **Nana:** The Newfoundland responsible for caring for the children in *Peter Pan*.
- **Old Yeller:** The Black Mouth Cur hunting dog who brings everyone to tears in the book of the same name.
- **Otis:** A pug that gets into playful hijinks in the movie *The Adventures of Milo and Otis*.
- **Rin-Tin-Tin:** A trained German Shepherd who was rescued from the battlefield in World War I and wound up staring in 27 films upon his return.
- **Santa's Little Helper:** A cartoon Greyhound on *The Simpsons*.

- **Shadow:** A wise Golden Retriever in the movie *Homeward Bound.*
- **Spot:** The infamous Bullmastiff from the *See Spot Run* books most children grow up reading.
- **Stella:** A French Bulldog who is treated just like one of the kids on *Modern Family.*

You may have noticed that some of those listed are actually the names of famous male dogs, but all could be used pretty interchangeably for your female pup. Not only is this because male names for females are rising in popularity, but also because there seems to be a different level of gender neutrality for dog names than humans. So if you want to name your little girl Otis, expect that some people might be confused, but don't allow that to sway your decision too much. If the name fits for your girl, that's all that matters.

Well, that and the fact that your kids will get a kick out of having a puppy named from one of their favorite dog movies.

Celebrity Dog Names

We've already discussed the ways that celebrities influence us every day, so why not take the names they are giving their dogs into consideration when choosing a name for your own pet?

In reality, most people won't make the automatic association if you give your puppy the same name Zoey Deschanel used. As inundated as we are by celebrity gossip, only hard-core fans go through life knowing off hand the name of their favorite celebrity's pet. So you could even use Justin Bieber's dog name and not worry too much about people thinking you are "copying" his choice. Most people simply won't notice or care.

And let's be honest; most celebrities got to where they are by being successful creatively. So it stands to reason that they might have something to teach us when it comes to naming our pets. At the very least, they can certainly provide some inspiration.

- **Asia:** French Bulldog owned by Lady Gaga
- **Bambi:** Chihuahua owned by Paris Hilton
- **Baylor:** Siberian Husky mix owned by Selena Gomez
- **Baxter:** Labrador mix owned by Ryan Reynolds
- **Bess:** Mixed breed owned by Sienna Miller
- **Biscuit:** French Bulldog owned by Travis Barker
- **Chewy:** Papillion owned by Christina Aguilera
- **Daisy:** Maltese/Toy Poodle mix owned by Jessica Simpson
- **Dot:** Mixed breed owned by Zoey Deschanel
- **Emu:** Shetland Sheepdog owned by Miley Cyrus
- **Esmeralda:** Labrador owned by Anne Hathaway
- **Finn:** Australian Shepherd mix owned by Amanda Seyfried
- **Flossie:** Chow-Chow/Labrador mix owned by Drew Barrymore
- **Francesca:** French Bulldog owned by Martha Stewart
- **Foxy:** Australian Cattle Dog owned by Matthew McConaughey
- **Frankie:** Yorkshire Terrier owned by Miranda Kerr
- **Harley:** Cavalier King Charles Spaniel owned by Julianne Hough
- **Honeychild:** Shih Tzu owned by Nicole Richie
- **Indo:** Rottweiler owned by Will Smith
- **Isaboo:** Pit Bull owned by Rachael Ray
- **Jinxy:** Maltese owned by Eva Longoria
- **Kola:** Mixed breed owned by Kellan Lutz
- **Lauren:** English Springer Spaniel owned by Oprah
- **Lexi:** Cavalier King Charles Spaniel owned by Julianne Hough
- **Lola:** Chihuahua owned by Hillary Duff

- **Lupo:** Cocker Spaniel owned by Prince William and Kate Middleton
- **Mimi LaRue:** Pug owned by Tori Spelling
- **Mona:** Boxer owned by Jennifer Love Hewitt
- **Noodles:** Pomeranian owned by Kelly Osbourne
- **Oprah:** Pug owned by Eva Longoria
- **Penny:** Maltese/Toy Poodle mix owned by Blake Lively
- **Poppy:** Chihuahua owned by Sandra Bullock
- **Ruby:** Chihuahua owned by Sandra Bullock
- **Sadie:** Cocker Spaniel owned by Oprah
- **Sammy:** Papillon owned by Justin Bieber
- **Scarlet:** French Bulldog owned by Victoria Beckham
- **Shadow:** Toy Poodle owned by Vanessa Hudgens
- **Sophie:** Maltese/Toy Poodle mix owned by Miley Cyrus
- **Sunny:** Springer Spaniel owned by Oprah
- **Tiffany:** Labrador mix owned by Joey Lawrence
- **Tina:** Pit Bull owned by Jessica Biel
- **Tinkerbell:** Chihuahua owned by Paris Hilton
- **Vida:** Chihuahua owned by Demi Moore
- **Zelda:** Mixed breed owned by Zoey Deschanel
- **Zoe:** Dachshund owned by Fergie and Josh Duhamel

Looking through that list, you probably noticed some of the trends we already discussed. Names based on physical characteristics, for instance, with a Chihuahua named Tinkerbell and a Maltese/Toy Poodle mix named Daisy – both smaller breeds with names arguably better suited for just that. There is also a Chewy in there, which could absolutely be indicative of an affinity for chewing – thus making that a name influenced by a personality trait.

So you see, even celebrities aren't immune to those name influencers we have already discussed. They, too, are subjected to the pull of those external forces leading them to the right name for their pet.

And if that right name then influences you towards the right name for *your* pet, even better.

Dogs Named After Celebrities

In the list of celebrity dog names, did you catch the pup named Oprah in there? Yes, that girl is owned by Eva Longoria – but she isn't the only dog in Hollywood named after the Queen of TV Talk. Rapper 50 Cent also has a Miniature Schnauzer with the same moniker.

That's not all, though. Ben Affleck and Jennifer Garner have a Labrador named Martha Stewart. Nick Jonas, of The Jonas Brothers, has a Golden Retriever named Elvis. And Reese Witherspoon named her French Bulldog after designer Coco Chanel.

As you can see, even celebrities are guilty of swooping up the names of their favorite famous peers and bestowing them upon their pets. They say that imitation is the best form of flattery, and these celebrities seemed more than willing to share their own fandom with the world by honoring the names of those they look up to.

Now, not everyone might consider it flattery. In fact, in some cases giving a real person's name to your dog could be considered a bit of a joke. Particularly if the name you choose (i.e. Brittany Spears) is one that has been in the news more frequently for crazy antics than reasons deserving of honor. But flattery or mockery, either way, celebrity names can prove to be a great resource when it comes to choosing a name for your own puppy.

One thing to keep in mind if you do opt for a celebrity name is that you may need to choose an abbreviated nickname when actually calling to your pup. As we discussed previously, dogs tend to respond better to shorter names, so anything with two words or multiple syllables might be too much.

But that doesn't mean you couldn't introduce your dog to others as Audrey Hepburn, while simply calling her Audrey at home. Think of this as being similar to first and last names for people. You don't routinely call your friends and family by their full names, and you don't have to call your pup by hers either.

What to Know When You Opt for Famous Inspiration

If your favorite movie growing up was *The Sandlot*, anytime you meet a dog named Hercules, you are automatically going to assume that the owner was also a fan of the same movie. But keep in mind that if you choose the name yourself, not everyone you meet is automatically going to make the association. That's because while the movie may have had an impact on you, it isn't necessarily one that has been seen or enjoyed by everyone.

This is true of a lot of famous or celebrity inspired names. How about a name from an actress, singer or TV film or book character? For those who do make the association, it can be a great conversation starter and shared joke. It may even open up doors for new friendships and relationships when you come across people who clearly have the same tastes in movies, literature and pop culture as you. But don't be disappointed if not everyone you meet "gets" the inspiration behind your name choice. Even with some of the most famous celebrity names, you may occasionally find yourself explaining where the name came from to people who aren't as up to date on current entertainment news as you are.

Another thing to keep in mind when naming your puppy after a celebrity is that celebrities are fallible, and their actions aren't always pretty. Someone at the top of her game today may seem like the perfect person to name your pup after, but we have all seen celebrities falter and fall, and anytime you name your pup after a real and living person, you run the risk of that person eventually doing something to incur the wrath of their previously adoring public.

34

Imagine the discomfort of anyone who named a pet OJ prior to the OJ Simpson murder scandals. That's just one example of how using a celebrity name could go very wrong. Obviously, that is a rare case, and not all celebrities will find themselves in such a negative light. But there is always the potential for drug and alcohol issues, as well as run-ins with the police. Some people may be totally fine with that, and even see the potential for a fall from grace as being part of the joke behind the name. But for others, especially those with kids, you may want to carefully consider the name you are choosing before elevating a celebrity to such an honored status in your home.

That said; if the name feels right for your puppy and seems to fit your personality and interests, go for it. Even if the celebrity you choose does eventually lose the preferred status they once held with you, you can always drop the full name and just introduce your pup to others by the shortened version you have been using all along at home.

Chapter 5: Names By Type: What to Name Your Cool, Funny, Cute, Exotic or Cultured Dog

If you haven't figured it out by now, there are literally thousands of names for you to choose from when it comes to christening your sweet girl with the perfect moniker. Which is probably exactly why you need a book like this – to help you wade through the choices and narrow down your options.

Doing that starts, first and foremost, with determining what kind of name you want. Are you hoping to inspire laughter upon puppy introductions, or would you rather a name that hints at sophistication and poise? Do you want a cool puppy name, or one that pays homage to your pup's heritage? Or maybe your main goal is simply to find a name that makes you feel all warm and fuzzy inside every time you say it.

There really are no wrong answers here, but choosing the right name has to start with first deciding what kind of name is going to appeal to you. So let's go over some of the possibilities, and hopefully you can pinpoint what category of names you prefer.

Cool Dog Names

What defines a "cool" dog name? Well, in reality, cool is a very subjective term. What's cool to you may not be cool to everyone else. But in general, there are some names that you can pretty much predict as being universally cool. Maybe that's because of the history these names hold, or because of the way they sound when we say them. Some names just have that spark that makes them seem destined for greatness. Whatever it is, these are the names that inspire a bit of awe whenever you hear them.

The names below are examples of those most people are likely to peg as being "cool". There are obviously plenty of cool dog names that didn't make the cut here, but look at this as a starting point – a way of helping you to decipher just what might make a name cool, giving you a reference point for the future.

- **Aphrodite:** The Greek Goddess of Love and Beauty, a name that certainly inspires reverence.
- **Aurora:** This name references the Northern Lights and Sleeping Beauty; both great inspirations to start from.
- **Azure:** The name of a gorgeous blue hue, this could be the perfectly cool name for your blue-eyed pup.
- **Brooklyn:** After one of the hippest places on the east coast.
- **Cadence:** A name that refers to rhythm, but also just has a very cool sound to it.

- **Cameo:** Picture a top actress popping in to steal the scene – does it get any cooler than that?
- **Cheyenne:** A Native American name that means to speak incoherently. This is one that mostly just sounds cool – and it is true to your pup, since you likely don't understand her barks.
- **Cleopatra:** You could call her Cleo for short, and honoring the Queen of the Nile is always a cool way to go.
- **Dahlia:** A beautiful name with a dark history, which is certainly a cool conversation starter.
- **Eden**: Yes, like the garden. Admit it, you kind of like the way it sounds rolling off your tongue.
- **Godiva:** Because who doesn't love this exclusive chocolate brand?
- **Indigo:** This name also lends well to a cool nickname: Indy.
- **Jade:** Perfect for your green-eyed pup, who is already cool in her own right.
- **Marilyn:** Yes, just like Monroe.
- **Opal:** If your puppy were a hipster…
- **Ophelia:** A cool name with classic literature roots, you could also easily call her Lia.
- **Pandora:** Everyone knows about Pandora's Box, but most people these days also relate Pandora to the popular music app.
- **Sookie:** If you haven't seen *True Blood*, you may not know why this name is so cool – but trust me, it is.
- **Wisteria:** Pop culture references are always cool.

Funny Dog Names

Plenty of people want to show off their sense of humor when introducing their dogs to strangers. And why not? This really is a great, consequence-free, way of infusing a little humor into your life. After all, unlike naming children, your dog isn't going to have to worry about facing humiliation in school or the workplace over an embarrassing name. You won't be judged a bad parent for giving your pup a name that wouldn't fit well in the professional world.

All your sweet girl is ever going to know is that her name was chosen lovingly and with care. So you have a little more leeway with puppy names when it comes to infusing your own unique sense of humor. But what is the best way to go about doing this?

There are three great tips to keep in mind when it comes to choosing a humorous dog name:

1. Titles are funny. Adding "Lady" or "Miss" to just about any name will somehow make it that much more humorous. You really can't go wrong.
2. Longer names are also hilarious. Giving your dog a full name, with 3 or 4 parts, is almost always funny. Obviously you will have to shorten that name when it comes to your day-to-day interactions with your pup. But for introductions, introducing your girl by her full name is sure to bring laughs, particularly if it is truly over the top.
3. Just one funny word can make all the difference. This applies to words that have funny meanings as well as to those that simply sound funny. Plug one into your puppy's name, and you probably have comedy gold.

Need some examples of what I'm talking about? Well, these are some great, humorous puppy names:

- **Chewbacca:** You can call her Chewy for short, but introducing her as Chewbacca will always draw big laughs.
- **Fussbucket:** For the puppy who is a bit needy, and the owner who likes to poke fun.
- **Lady Prissy Kissy:** Silly and with the title of Lady. Plus, it's fun to say. Although, you will likely want to shorten it to Lady or Kissy for the sake of your pup.
- **Mindy Fluffer Nutter:** It means nothing. But it sure would be funny to say.

39

- **Miss Kitty:** Obviously, she's not a cat. And that's exactly why it's funny.
- **Peanut Wigglebutt:** Anytime you can add "butt" into a name, kids will think it's funny for sure.
- **Puddles A. Lot:** Because sometimes puppies have accidents. And making fun of that, instead of getting angry, is always the preferable option.
- **Punky Chewster:** Just like Punky Brewster. Only funnier.
- **Ruffles Ms. Truffles:** Calling her Truffles for short would be advisable, but for everyone who knows her full name – there will be plenty of giggles.
- **Sergeant Gumdrop:** For the pup who exudes leadership abilities in chasing and cuteness.
- **Twyla Punkin Twinkeltoes:** See. Longer names are almost always funny. In fact, perhaps we should all give our pups full names, just for the laughs.
- **Queen Stink:** You'll probably just want to call her Queen, or Queenie, but when you introduce her to others – use her full name and expect the laughs that ensue.
- **Whoopi:** Whether you're referencing whoopee cushions or Whoopi Goldberg, you know it's funny.

Cute Dog Names

Cute puppy names, especially, are a limitless commodity. Really, just about any puppy name you come across could be designated in the cute category. At least, all names that aren't intentionally meant to be fierce.

Still, it could be argued that some names are more adorable than others. I tend to think names that could otherwise be used as pet names between couples are great examples of this. Just take a look for yourself:

- **Baby:** Chances are, you're already treating her just like your baby. So calling her Baby may just be a natural extension of that relationship.
- **Biscuit:** If your pup is a miniature or toy version, Biscuit could be the perfectly adorable name for her you have been looking for.
- **Cinnabun:** A sweet name for a sweet girl.
- **Honey:** For your caramel colored pet, Honey might just be one of the cutest names you'll find.
- **Lovie:** Often, a child's favorite stuffed animal is referred to as his or her lovie. Which may be exactly why this makes such a great name for a beloved pet.
- **Love Bug:** This is just a sweet name that is always fun to say.
- **Princess:** Because let's face it, she is your princess – and it's cute to refer to her as such.
- **Sweetie:** This is one pet name that is sure to inspire "awwws".
- **Twinkle Toes:** She may not be a world-class dancer, but she is probably still always dancing at your feet.

Exotic Dog Names

As we've already discussed, having a foreign breed dog opens up a great opportunity to give your pup a unique and exotic name. So many breeds have exotic origins, and in those cases, there is a whole other realm of name possibilities to consider:

Spanish Breeds (Chihuahua, Mexican Hairless, Spanish Mastiff, etc.)

- **Bonita:** The Spanish word for beautiful, and the perfect fit for your gorgeous pup.
- **Charo:** This is the Spanish nickname for Rosa, an ideal fit for your little flower.

- **Chiquita:** Just think, you could call her Chicky for short.
- **Esmerelda:** For the Spanish emerald in your life.
- **Isabella:** A revered queen of Spain; making this a great name for the little queen in your world.
- **Madre:** The Spanish word for mother, this might be a great fit for any dog you plan on eventually breeding.
- **Margarita:** Not only is this one of your favorite drinks, it also means pearl – perfectly suited for your feisty and precious girl.
- **Patagonia:** A gorgeous region in South America, and a name that can easily be shortened to Nia.
- **Rosalinda:** For the prettiest little rose you know.

Russian Breeds (Black Russian Terrier, East Siberian Laika, Russian Spaniel, Siberian Husky, etc.)

- **Anastasia:** In Russian, this name means reborn. Not only is it a beautiful name, but it could also be meaningful for a family who is getting a puppy after the loss of another pet.
- **Angara:** A Siberian river, and a great name for your pup.
- **Anya:** The Russian variation of Anna.
- **Babushka:** In Russian, this is an older woman or grandmother.
- **Irina:** This name translates into peace, and could be the perfect fit for your sweet and sedated girl.
- **Ivana:** A popular Russian name that is the female version of Ivan – meaning, the terrible. This could be a great fit for your ornery pup.
- **Pavlova:** This is a name that honors one of the greatest Russian ballet dancers, but it also tips a hat at Pavlov's dogs, perhaps the most famous laboratory dogs of all time.
- **Samara:** A Russian river and a truly unique and beautiful name.

- **Zoya:** The name that translates literally into life, and since your new puppy is the light of your life – it could be the perfect fit.

German Breeds (Bavarian Mountain Hound, Dachshund, German Shepherd, Miniature Pinscher, Pomeranian, etc.)

- **Adelaide:** In German, this name means noble and serene – a great fit for your well-behaved girl.
- **Ava:** This popular German name means bird, but it's also just a very pretty name to say.
- **Bernadette:** Meaning brave as a bear, this could be a great name for your fierce pup who thinks she's bigger than she is.
- **Carolyn:** Like a melody or song, this name is perfect for your pup who likes to exercise her vocal chords.
- **Gertrude:** The beloved warrior, this might be just the name for you if your pup is destined to be the guardian of your house.
- **Greta:** A perfectly German name for a perfectly German pup.
- **Helga:** This may not be the sweetest name to say, but it will certainly conjure up German imagery for all those who hear it.
- **Mathilda:** A name that translates into battle maiden, this is another great fit for the pup you intend to be a protector.
- **Selma:** The divine protector – apparently a lot of German puppy names are perfect for guard dogs.
- **Winifred:** This one means peaceful friend – great for your sweet pup who just wants to be by your side.

Scottish Breeds (Bearded Collie, Terrier, Golden Retriever, etc.)

- **Ainsley:** Meaning "one's own meadow", which isn't necessarily a great fit for a pup, but it sure is pretty to say.
- **Alpina:** Meaning blond, this is the perfect name for your fair-haired Scottish pup.
- **Annabella:** For your puppy with beautiful grace in spades.
- **Bonnie:** The word for beautiful that may just be perfectly suit for your girl.
- **Duffy:** In Scotland, duff means black – so Duffy could be a great name for your dark haired pup.
- **Mackenzie:** A beautiful name that can be easily shortened to Kenzie.
- **Maggie:** This one would be a great fit for both Scottish and Irish breeds.
- **Tyra:** Meaning land, this name could translate perfectly for your pup who is always roaming.

Cultured Dog Names

Perhaps the point you really want to get across with your puppy name is that you are high class and cultured. In that case, there are plenty of names to choose from that are plucked straight out of literature, art, design and music.

Maybe you want to name your pup after your favorite artist, or there might be a character in a classic novel that you have always admired. The beauty of a cultured name is that it is a great way for you to express your interests to the world, and it can open up a variety of conversations with the likeminded people you come across when introducing your pup. Those who immediately pick up on the origin of your little girl's name are going to be the same people you will want to spend your time getting to know further.

The only real goal with a cultured name is to express your more cultured interests, but those will vary greatly from person to person.

Still, these are a few names that may be exactly what you are looking for:

- **Cashmere:** Just like the fabric, this is a cute and trendy name for your high-class pup.
- **Chantilly:** A quality lace whose name is a great fit for a quality girl.
- **Chanel:** After the designer, of course.
- **Jane Austen:** For the acclaimed writer who has become a bit of a pop culture icon in her own right.
- **Liza Minnelli:** Liza for short. Arguably one of the best Broadway divas of all time.
- **Mona Lisa:** For the famous painting of the same name.
- **Versace:** Another fashion inspired name that exudes high-end confidence.

What Type is Right For You?

Hopefully by now, you are growing more and more aware of what it is you are looking for in a name. At the end of this book, you will be faced with an exhaustive list of potential puppy names, and this knowledge will help you to weed through those names and decipher the possibilities you are actually interested in from the names that just wouldn't work for you.

So what is it? Do you see yourself with a humorous puppy name? A cultured one? A name befitting of your dog's heritage? Or something else?

What kind of feelings do you want your puppy's name to invoke?

Once you figure that out, you'll find that you are that much closer to the perfect name you seek.

Chapter 6: Naming by Physical Characteristics

We've already discussed so many ways to choose your puppy's name, but we have saved perhaps the most obvious for last. The names that should pop into mind automatically just by looking at your pup.

Whether she is small and brown, or large with blue eyes – I can guarantee you there is a name that perfectly aligns with her looks. In fact, there are probably several; so many name possibilities that directly reflect your girl's physical characteristics. You really can't go wrong.

A lot of these names may overlap. For instance, you might find that some of the names on the list for white dogs are also impeccably suited for small pups. That's actually a good thing – it means you can find a name that perfectly describes your girl. After all, if you can hit upon several of her physical characteristics in the same name, isn't that even better than just describing one?

In life, we don't often get to bestow names that seem like they were meant just for the person we are picking them for. That's because people don't typically show us who they are in infancy – and naming based on physical characteristics for a person might be looked down upon. But with dogs, there are a lot of options for finding exactly that – a name that feels like a perfect fit. And sometimes, naming based on physical characteristics is the best way to accomplish that.

So let's go over some examples and give you an idea of the many directions you have to go when it comes to anointing your pup with a name that is meant to fit her looks. You might just come to realize that these are the names you were looking for all along.

Big Dogs

There are a lot of big breed pups that are deserving of names as large and in charge as they are. German Shepherds, Rottweilers, St. Bernards, Greyhounds, Mastiffs; these just start off the list. If your puppy is going to grow into a big girl, you can look forward to having a hiking partner and guard dog that will always stand by your side. And there isn't much cuter then giant puppy paws on a girl who still seems so small – the real indicator of the size she is going to grow into.

So what do you name that large partner in crime of yours? Well, you have two options – going big, or going funny. Because when it comes to big dog names, you can either use those meant to implicate the size of your pup, or you can choose a small dog name in an attempt to procure laughs. Let me show you what I mean:

- **Alaska:** A name from the biggest state, it makes perfect sense for your big girl.
- **Banshee:** A female spirit in Irish mythology known as being a messenger from the underworld – this is one tough girl.
- **Cadi:** An abbreviated version of Cadillac, certainly fitting for your big pup.
- **Dozer:** Just like a giant piece of machinery, your little Dozer isn't quite so little after all.
- **Luxe:** Short for Deluxe – your super-sized pet.
- **Pixie:** Because like I said, sometimes there is humor in giving your big girl a name that clearly depicts anything but large.
- **Queen:** Let's face it, she is obviously already the queen of her castle. And by default, yours.
- **Zephyr:** A name that means fast moving train, this could be the perfect fit for your big girl who navigates her world with force and speed.

Little Pups

Let's just say that when you were picking out a pup, you were looking for more of a lap dog. You want your girl to be your companion and cuddle bug, which means that you probably chose a Chihuahua, Terrier, Beagle, Cavalier King Charles Spaniel, Dachshund, or one of the many other breeds that is known for being small. The kind of dog you could carry around in your purse if you wanted, and the girl you fully intend on treating just like a princess.

As with the big dog names listed above, you have a choice with small puppies – you can either choose a name that clearly indicates her diminutive size, or you can go for laughs and choose one of the big dog names we've already discussed. Because a Chihuahua named Dozer is really quite funny. If you want to go small, though, here are some examples of names you might choose.

- **Bitsy:** For the cute little bit in your life.
- **Buttercup:** The name of a gorgeous yellow flower, this one just automatically brings to mind a little puppy.
- **Gizmo:** Remember the good gremlin in the movie *Gremlins*? That's where this name comes from, and it couldn't be more perfectly suited for your sweet girl.
- **Keiki:** This one actually means "child" in Hawaiian, making it a great fit for your little one.
- **Minnie:** Just like the mouse, only this name refers precisely to your puppy's size.
- **Pixie:** Yes, this name was ironically on the big dog list as well – but for your small pup, it's here because it actually fits.
- **Pippin:** If you're a *Lord of the Rings* fan, you will remember Pippin as being one of the curious Hobbits who had a knack for trouble – perhaps a great description for your girl.
- **Pookie:** This is one of those names that is just so sugary sweet, it has to be for a small pup.
- **Squirt:** Precisely the name a big brother might call his kid sister, this one is a great fit for *your* little Squirt.

White Dogs

For dogs with a snowy complexion, finding a name that suits them is easier then you might think. Breeds like American Eskimos, Bichon Frises, and White Highland Terriers all boast the white fur that sets them apart and makes them unique beauties deserving of uniquely beautiful names.

- **Alpine:** A name straight out of the snow-covered north, this could be just the moniker you're looking for.
- **Avalanche:** You could call her Ava for short, but you would always know her name was inspired by a whole lot of snow.
- **Bianca:** It means white in Italian – a name that is beautiful and fitting.

- **Casper:** You could always call her Cassy, still giving a nod to the little white ghost.
- **Cotton Ball:** It's adorable and fitting, especially for your little ball of fur.
- **Denali:** This is a National Park in Alaska that is almost always snow-capped.
- **Ivory:** The name is self-explanatory, but it sure does have a pretty ring to it, right?
- **Marshmallow:** This one could be especially perfect for your chubby pup.
- **Popcorn:** Is your girl constantly jumping around like corn out of the popper? Then her coloring and personality may make her perfectly suited for this name.
- **Powder Puff:** This sweet name is a great fit for your small white pup.
- **Snow White:** Just like the Disney Princess. This one is even more fun if you start naming all your other pets after the seven dwarfs.
- **Stardust:** A pretty name for a special girl.

Brown Pups

There are plenty of breeds that have brown puppies in their line, but some more common examples might be Bloodhounds, Chocolate Labradors and Irish Setters. Let's face it, brown dogs aren't exactly unique – but that doesn't mean their names can't still be special. Some ideas for your chocolate hued girl might include:

- **Almond Joy:** You could call her Joy for short, but this might be the perfect way to pay homage to your favorite candy bar.
- **Brownie:** So obvious, so sweet, so perfect.
- **Cappuccino:** A great nickname for this one is Cappy, and it is perfect for a coffee-loving owner.

- **Cocoa Puff:** Anytime you add Puff to a name, it inspires thoughts of a miniature little fur ball – so this could be a great fit for your small brown pup.
- **Hershey:** The popular chocolate brand might actually be the perfect name for your sweet girl.
- **Kisses:** Just like the Hershey Kisses we all adore.
- **Muffin:** It's one of those sweet pet names that could also be classically suited for a chocolate-hued pup.
- **Nutella:** If you are already obsessed with this hazelnut spread, it might be exactly the name you're looking for.
- **Peanut:** A name that could also easily go on our small dog list.
- **Snickers:** Let's face it, brown pups are just begging for a chocolate treat name.
- **Tawny:** This is a beautiful and unique name that is perfect you're your espresso colored girl.

Black Dogs

Along the same lines, there are black dogs in many different breeds, but some you might come across include Bernese Mountain Dogs, Doberman Pinschers and certain Terriers. For your girl with black fur, some of these names might be the perfect fit:

- **Blackberry:** Fruit names are always fun for female pups.
- **Blackbird:** Completely fitting for your dark haired girl.
- **Black Beauty:** This could be an especially great name for families with kids who love horses. Let them hear the story of Black Beauty and they are sure to fall in love with the name.
- **Checkers:** A fun and unique name that could set your girl apart.
- **Ebony:** This is a classy name for your sophisticated girl.

- **Elvira:** For those who remember the Mistress of the Dark, this could be a great fit.
- **Indigo:** This is one of those cool names we discussed that just *sounds* special.
- **Magpie:** A unique variation of Maggie that will automatically inspire visions of your dark haired pup.
- **Midnight:** Perhaps your girl is a bit of a night owl as well, making this name even more perfectly suited.
- **Onyx:** A beautiful name for a dark pup.
- **Raven:** Another bird name that could be a great fit for your girl.
- **Twilight:** For those moments just as the dark settles in, this could also easily be shortened to Twyla.

Red or Orange Pups

You can find red Dachshunds and Spaniels, and Ridgeback puppies are also often red or orange in coloring, but they certainly aren't the only breeds that boast this coloring. Still, these girls are often considered unique and special because of their hue, and they are deserving of names that reflect just that:

- **Amber:** A dark orange coloring that you might find in glassware or fossilized resin, it is very pretty and could be exactly the right fit you are looking for.
- **Autumn:** Just like the changing leaves of fall, this name automatically conjures up images of reds and oranges.
- **Cinnamon:** A popular spice that boasts that reddish brown hue you might see in your pup's fur.
- **Chianti:** Perfect for wine lovers who have a special place in their hearts for reds.
- **Gingersnap:** A sweet cookie that could perfectly fit your auburn girl.
- **Lucy:** In honor of Lucille Ball, perhaps one of the first redheaded stars of the small screen.

- **Nutmeg:** Another spice name that is known for that reddish brown coloring.
- **Pumpkin Head:** Fun and obvious.
- **Scarlet:** Straight out of *Gone with the Wind*, this name also points exclusively to the color red.

Blond Dogs

Plenty of breeds have blond puppies as well, but some of the most common might include Golden Retrievers, Afghan Hounds and Cocker Spaniels. They say that blonds have more fun, and that could certainly be true of your pup with names like this:

- **Blondie:** Doesn't this one seem pretty obvious?
- **Butterscotch:** For the sweet treat that offers up a lighter hue.
- **Ditzy:** So, this one is poking a little fun at blonds, but if you can have a sense of humor about it – so can your dog.
- **Goldie:** Just like Goldie Hawn, this name automatically makes people think of blonds.
- **Honeysuckle:** Because referencing honey is a great way to go when naming your blond pup.
- **Sandy:** People often refer to blonds as having a sandy hair coloring, so this could be the perfect fit for your girl.
- **Sunshine:** Just like the bright sun shining down on us from above, this name might just fit her personality and her fur.

Spotted Pups

Most people think of Dalmatians when they think of spotted dogs, but they aren't the only ones to carry these unique markings. American Hairless Terriers and Old Danish Pointers are also known for having spots. And while Spot can be an obvious name for these dogs, it certainly isn't your only option. When it comes to naming spotted pups, some of these might work perfectly:

- **Bootsie:** Especially perfect if her markings extend to her paws like boots.
- **Dice:** Because her spots may just make her look like a pair of dice.
- **Dottie:** A fun and fitting name for your spotted girl who is also a little kooky.
- **Freckles:** Because even though her spots aren't actually freckles, the name still feels like it fits.
- **Oreo:** For your black and white spotted girl who totally reminds you of the cookies you adore.
- **Speckles:** A sweet name with obvious connotations.

Blue Eyed Dogs

Siberian Huskies and Australian Shepherds are both known for having strikingly blue eyes. And when you have eyes that stand out, a name to go along with them is always fitting.

- **Azure:** A gorgeous name that fits perfectly for your girl with eyes the color of the sky.
- **Blue:** Or Blueberry. Really, any name that utilizes the color blue could work. And they are all so cute.
- **Cobalt:** Directly referring to that brilliant blue color.
- **Sapphire:** A beautiful name that might just fit her perfectly.
- **Skye:** Because that is exactly what her eyes remind you of.

When Looks Matter

So you see, there are a lot of options when it comes to naming your girl based purely on her looks. The good news is, doing just that certainly isn't as looked down upon with pups as it might be for babies. You can easily give your puppy a name that is directly representative of her looks, and no one will bat an eye. In fact, they might actually commend you on creatively incorporating her looks and her name.

You just have to decide if that's the direction you want to go. Or if you would rather pursue one of the other naming options we have already discussed?

Either way, you're about to be inundated by a whole lot of naming options. If you don't have a name after this, you might just have to send her back.

Just kidding, of course, but your perfect name is out there – now we just have to find it.

Chapter 7: Top 500 Female Dog Names

1. **Abby:** Origin: Biblical; Meaning: My Father is Joy; Variations: Abbie, Abigail
2. **Addie:** Origin: French; Meaning: Noble and Kind; Variations: Addison, Adelaide, Adele
3. **Adele:** Origin: French; Meaning: Good Humor; Variation: Adelle; Famous Namesake: Musician Adelle
4. **Aida:** Origin: Arabic; Meaning: Returning Visitor; Variation: Ayda
5. **Airabell:** Origin: Scottish; Meaning: Invokable; Variation: Arabella
6. **Aggy:** Origin: Slang; Meaning: Aggravating; Great for hyper dogs and sarcastic owners.
7. **Alex:** Origin: Greek Mythology; Meaning: Defender; Variations: Alexis, Alexandra
8. **Ali:** Origin: Arabic; Meaning: Lofty and Sublime; Variations: Allie, Aliya
9. **Alice:** Origin: French; Meaning, Kind
10. **Alma:** Origin: Latin; Meaning: Nourishing
11. **Alyssa:** Origin: Latin; Meaning: Noble; Variations: Alicia, Alise
12. **Amber:** Origin: English; Meaning: Gemstone; Great for dogs with red hair; Variation: Amberly
13. **Amelia:** Origin: German; Meaning: Work; Variations: Amelie, Amalia
14. **Amy:** Origin: English; Meaning: Beloved; Variation: Amee
15. **Anastasia:** Origin: Latin and Greek; Meaning: Resurrection
16. **Angel:** Origin: Latin; Meaning: Messenger; Great for your sweet, angelic girl.
17. **Angie:** Origin: Greek; Meaning: Angel or Messenger; Variation: Angela
18. **Anika:** Origin: German, Dutch, Danish and Slovene; Meaning: Grace; Variation: Annika
19. **Anna:** Origin: New Testament; Meaning: Gracious and Merciful; Variations: Annabelle, Anne, Annie
20. **Annemarie:** Origin: German; Meaning: Bitter Grace; Great for your sassy pup.

21. **Anya:** Origin: Russian; Meaning: Favor and Grace; Great for your sweet Russian breed pup, like Siberian Huskies and Russian Terriers.
22. **Applejack:** Origin: American Cereal Brand; Nickname: Apple; Great for excitable breeds.
23. **Apricot:** Origin: Fruit; Great for lighter hued breeds with sweet dispositions.
24. **April:** Origin: Latin; Meaning: To Open; Fun Fact: This name has only been in circulation since the 1940's.
25. **Aria:** Origin: Italian; Meaning: Song or Melody; Nickname: Ary
26. **Arianna:** Origin: Greek; Meaning: Most Holy; Variation: Ariadne
27. **Ariel:** Origin: Hebrew; Meaning: Lion of God; Fun Fact: Shakespeare use the name Ariel in his play *The Tempest*, but it didn't become popular until it was used in 1989's The *Little Mermaid*.
28. **Ashley:** Origin: English; Meaning: Ash Tree Clearing; Nickname: Ash; Fun Fact: Until the 1960's, this was primarily a boys name, but now it is used mostly for girls.
29. **Aspen:** Origin: English; Derived From: Aspen Trees; Great for your cold weather breeds.
30. **Athena:** Origin: Greek Mythology; Meaning: Wisdom and warfare; Variation: Athene
31. **Aubree:** Origin: English; Meaning: Fair Ruler of the Little People; Variation: Aubrey
32. **Audrey:** Origin: English; Meaning: Noble and Strength; Fun Fact: This name will always be associated with the 1900's actress, Audrey Hepburn. Great for your glamorous pup.
33. **Auggie:** Origin: Roman and German; Meaning: Great and Magnificent; Variation: August
34. **Autumn:** Origin: Latin; Meaning: The Fall Season; Great for your fall-born pups, or those with fur the color of autumn leaves.
35. **Ava:** Origin: Latin; Meaning: Life; Variations: Avi, Aveline

36. **Avery:** Origin: French; Meaning: Counsel; Nickname: Avy
37. **Azzurra:** Origin: Italian; Meaning: Sky Blue; Variation: Azure
38. **Babe:** Origin: Latin; Meaning: Foreign Woman; Variation: Barbara
39. **Babs:** Origin: Greek; Meaning: Foreign; Variation: Barbara; Fun Fact: Barbara Streisand fans have long since claimed Babs as her nickname of honor, so this is a great puppy name for fans of Streisand's work.
40. **Babushka:** Origin: Russian; Meaning: Granny; Great for your pup with a wise and old soul.
41. **Baby:** We all know what "baby" means. And there is a good chance you will be calling your sweet pup "baby" no matter what you name her. So perhaps you want to consider going with the obvious for her name.
42. **Bacon:** Similarly, you could go for humor by naming your pup "Bacon". After all, who doesn't love bacon? A great name for your pup with a big appetite.
43. **Bailey:** Origin: Middle English; Meaning: Bailiff; Variations: Bailee, Baylee
44. **Bambi:** Origin: Italian; Meaning: Young Girl; Great for Disney fans who are already twitterpated with their little pup.
45. **Basil:** Origin: Greek; Meaning: Royalty; Great for pups that are always following you around in the kitchen.
46. **Bean:** Origin: Scottish; Meaning: Fair Skinned; Great for small pups who will never grow more than a few pounds.
47. **Bear:** There is always something fun and cute about naming your pup after another animal. For your fierce little girl who thinks she's bigger than she is, Bear could be the perfect moniker.
48. **Beatrice:** Origin: Italian; Meaning: Voyager or Traveler; Variation: Beatrix
49. **Bee:** Origin: Latin; Meaning: She Who Brings Happiness; Variation: Bea

50. **Bella:** Origin: Italian; Meaning: Beautiful; Variations: Belle, Bell
51. **Berty:** Origin: French; Meaning: Intelligent; Variation: Bertie
52. **Bessie:** Origin: Greek; Meaning: My God is An Oath or My God is Abundance; Variations: Bessy, Elizabeth
53. **Betsy:** Origin: English; Meaning: God is Satisfaction; Variation: Betty; Fun Fact: This is the Americanized version of Elizabeth or Bessie.
54. **Billie Jean:** Billie Jean is a name directly from a Michael Jackson song. If you are a fan of the King of Pop, your new pup might benefit from a name straight out of one of your favorite songs.
55. **Bindi:** Origin: Indian (Sanskrit); Meaning: A Drop; Nickname: Bin, Binny
56. **Birdie:** Origin: English; Meaning: Little Bird, Birdlike; Variation: Birdy
57. **Biscuit:** This can be a cute name for your pup, without much of a deeper meaning. Maybe you just like biscuits. Either way, it is the perfect name for a smaller breed.
58. **Bitsy:** Origin: English; Great for small and sassy breeds.
59. **Bizzy:** The perfect name for your hyper and easily excitable pup.
60. **Blackberry:** Maybe you want to name your pup after one of your favorite fruits. Blackberry is a great name for darker pups.
61. **Blaze:** Origin: English; Meaning: Lisping; Variation: Blaise
62. **Blondie:** Origin: English; Great for your blond or lighter-haired pup.
63. **Blossom** Origin: English; Meaning: Fresh
64. **Blue:** Origin: English; Meaning: Sad or the Color Blue; Variation: Blueberry
65. **Bo:** Origin: Swedish, Danish; Meaning: To Live; Variation: Bobo
66. **Boffin:** Origin: British; Meaning: Scientist; Great for the scientifically inclined pet owner.

67. **Bonbon:** Bonbons are a sweet treat that are often joked about being a favorite of housewives. This could be the perfect name for a stay-at-home pet owner looking for a sweet companion.

68. **Bonnie:** Origin: Scottish; Meaning: Pretty; Fun Fact: This name became especially popular after it was featured as the name of Scarlett's daughter in *Gone with the Wind*.

69. **Boo:** Origin: English Pop Culture; Variation: BooBoo; Fun Fact: This has become a popular term for denoting one's love in pop and rap music.

70. **Boots:** A great name for a pup that has different colored fur on their legs and feet from the rest of their body.

71. **Bows:** A sweet name for the puppy you plan on adorning in bows as often as possible.

72. **Brandy:** Origin: English Alcoholic Drink; Meaning: Burnt Wine; Variation: Brandee

73. **Brooke:** Origin: English; Meaning: Lives by the Stream; Variation: Brook

74. **Brooklyn:** Origin: Borough in New York City; Meaning: Broken Land

75. **Brownie:** Everyone loves a brownie. So for your sweet pup, perhaps with chocolate coloring, this could be the perfect name.

76. **Bubblegum:** For your pup who is full of energy and pep, Bubblegum might be exactly the name you are looking for.

77. **Bubbles:** If you have kids, you know how much they love Bubbles — so what could be more perfect than naming your new female pup after one of their favorite attractions.

78. **Buffy:** Origin: Hebrew; Meaning: Pledged to God; Fun Fact: Buffy became a popular name after the show *Buffy the Vampire Slayer*.

79. **Bunny:** Origin: Latin; Meaning: To Bring or Victory;

80. **Buttercup:** The name of a flower, Buttercup might appeal to you if you are a fan of *The Princess Bride*, where the coveted princess boasted this moniker.

81. **Butternut:** Sometimes, you just want to give your dog a cutesy name that is also a food. If that sounds like you, Butternut may be the right name for your new pup.

82. **Butterscotch:** A lovable pup deserves an equally sugary-sweet name, and your fair-haired 4-legged friend may be perfectly suited for the name Butterscotch.

83. **Button:** Maybe your sweet girl is as cute as a button. If so, why not name her as such?

84. **Cadence:** Origin: English; Meaning: Rhythm or Flow; Variation: Kaydence

85. **Cairo:** Origin: City in Egypt; Meaning: The Victorious; Great for breeds like the Pharaoh Hound.

86. **Callie:** Origin: English; Meaning: Lark or The Most Beautiful; Nickname: Call

87. **Candy:** Origin: English; Meaning: Queen Mother; Variation: Candace

88. **Cappuccino:** Is your pup hyper and chocolate colored? If so, Cappuccino might be just the fitting name you are looking for. You could even call her "Cappy" for short.

89. **Caramel:** Yum. Everyone loves caramel, and this name is perfect for your sweet, caramel-colored girl.

90. **Carly:** Origin: English; Meaning: Small Champion; Variations: Carlene, Carley, Carlie

91. **Carmela:** Origin: Italian and Spanish; Meaning: Garden; Variation: Carmelita

92. **Carmen:** Origin: Spanish; Meaning: Song; Variation: Carmina

93. **Cassie:** Origin: Greek; Meaning: Shining Upon Man; Variation: Cassandra

94. **CeCe:** Origin: Latin; Meaning: Blind One; Variations: Cici, Cecilia, Cecily

95. **Cha-Cha:** Love to dance and have a pup that is always moving with you? Then Cha-Cha might be the right name for you.

96. **Chantilly:** Origin: French; Meaning: Lace; Nickname: Tilly

97. **Charlie:** Origin: German; Meaning: Warrior; Variations: Charley, Charlene
98. **Charlotte:** Origin: French; Meaning: Feminine of Charles, Which Means Manly; Nickname: Lotty
99. **Chelsea:** Origin: District in London; Meaning: Landing Place for Chalk or Limestone; Variations: Chelsey, Chelsie
100. **Cherub:** The name of an angel, Cherub could be exactly what your sweet pup is hoping to be called.
101. **Cherry:** Origin: English; Meaning: Generous Love
102. **Chew-Chew:** A fun name for a pup that always has something in her mouth, Chew-Chew or Chewy could be exactly the right fit you are looking for.
103. **Chi Chi:** Origin: Modern Slang; Meaning: Showily or Affectedly Elegant or Trendy
104. **China:** Origin: Asian Country; Variation: Chi; Great for Asian breeds, like the Chinese Crested or Kintamani.
105. **Chippy:** Do you have a chipper pet that maybe even has spots like a chocolate chip cookie? If so, Chippy may be just the name you're looking for.
106. **Chloe:** Origin: Greek; Meaning: Green Shoot; Variations: Khloe, Cloe
107. **Chocolate:** Everyone knows Chocolate is a treat most women can't do without. So why not give your new pup a name fitting of your favorite sweet indulgence?
108. **Cinderella:** Origin: English; Meaning: Little Ashes
109. **Cindy:** Origin: Greek; Meaning: Woman from Kynthos; Variation: Cynthia
110. **Cinnamon:** This popular spice name can be the perfect pick for your red haired pup.
111. **Claire:** Origin: French; Meaning: Clear and Bright; Nickname: Claire-Bear
112. **Clara:** Origin: Italian; Meaning: Bright
113. **Cleo:** Origin: Greek; Meaning: Glory; Variation: Cleopatra
114. **Clover:** Origin: Flower Name; Good for your perky pup who you want to give a unique flower name to.

115. **Coco:** Origin: French; Variation:, Cocoa; Fun Fact: Coco Chanel popularized this name, which means that anointing your pup with this moniker could be a great way to show off your love of fashion.

116. **Coconut:** The perfect name for your snow-white puppy.

117. **Cookie:** Origin: English; Meaning: Sweet Biscuit

118. **Copper:** If you want to name your new puppy after a precious metal, this could be the right choice for your brown or red-haired pet.

119. **Cora:** Origin: Greek; Meaning: Maiden; Variation: Corinna

120. **Coral:** Origin: English; Good for pet owners who have a love of the sea.

121. **Cordelia:** Origin: Celtic; Meaning: Of the Sea

122. **Cotton:** Is your pup a fluffy white fur-ball? If so, what name could be better suited for her then Cotton?

123. **Cricket:** This is a fun and unique name that is starting to make a comeback in popularity. Maybe Cricket is the right choice for your pup.

124. **Cuddles:** Origin: Scottish; Meaning: Donkey; Nickname: Cuddy

125. **Cupcake:** Another sweet treat name that could be perfect for your new pup.

126. **Cutie:** Let's face it, you were calling her Cutie from the first time she licked your face. Might as well make it official with her name.

127. **Curly:** Perfect for the pup with locks of curly fur.

128. **Daisy:** Origin: English; Meaning: White Flower; Nickname, Daisy Duke

129. **Dakota:** Origin: Native American; Meaning: Allies or Friends; Nickname: Kota

130. **Dallas:** Origin: English; Meaning: Meadow Dwelling; Good for pet owners who want to honor the state of Texas.

131. **Dancer:** Is dancing your passion? Then why not combine your two loves, and name your sweet girl after your favorite pastime.

132. **Danica:** Origin: Slavic; Meaning: Morning Star or Venus; Variation: Danika

133. **Daphne:** Origin: Greek; Meaning: Laurel; Variations: Dafina, Dafne

134. **Dawn:** Origin: English; Meaning: Awakening

135. **Dee Dee:** Origin: English; Meaning: Beloved; Variation: Didi

136. **Delilah:** Origin: Biblical; Meaning: Delicate, Weak and Languishing; Nickname: Lila

137. **Delphi:** Origin: Greek; Meaning: The Most Important Oracle in ancient Greece; Variation: Delphine

138. **Derby:** If you have a feeling your new pup is constantly competing in a race of her own, always running around the house, Derby might just be the appropriate name to call her.

139. **Diamond:** Origin: Colorless and Precious Stone; Meaning: Invincible and Untamed; Everyone knows diamonds are a girl's best friend, so why not give your pup a name fitting of her new place in your life?

140. **Dido:** Origin: Roman Mythology; Meaning: Virgin

141. **Diva:** Perhaps your new girl is already exhibiting some diva-like qualities, or maybe you just intend on treating her as such. Either way, Diva can be the perfect name for your new little love.

142. **Dixie:** Origin: English; Meaning: Southern United States; Nickname: Dix

143. **Dizzy:** A lot of puppies seem to lack the coordination of their older counterparts, and some are destined to always be a little loopy. If you suspect your pup may be one of those, Dizzy could be a fun way to honor her uniqueness in name.

144. **Dolly:** Origin: English; Meaning: A Vision; Variation: Dollie

145. **Doodle:** Origin: English; Variation: Doodle-Bug

146. **Dora:** Origin: English; Meaning: Gift; Good for pet owners with kids who love *Dora the Explorer*.

147. **Dorothy:** Origin: English; Meaning: Gift of God; Variation: Dorothea

148. **Dottie:** Origin: English; Meaning: Gift; Variations: Dot, Dotty

149. **Duchess:** A name befitting royalty, Duchess may be the way to go for your pampered pet.

150. **Duffy:** Origin: Gaelic; Meaning: Dark Skinned

151. **Dusty:** Origin: English; Meaning: Brave Soldier

152. **Eartha:** Origin: English; Meaning: Worldly; Famous Namesake: Eartha Kitt

153. **Echo:** Origin: Greek; Meaning: Sound; Good for your yappy pup who is always testing the strength of her own voice.

154. **Eire:** Origin: Gaelic; Meaning: Gaelic Goddess of the Land

155. **Eleanor:** Origin: English; Meaning: Shining Light; Nickname: Lenor, Nora

156. **Elf:** Want a cute name for your Christmas-time pup? She might just be your perfect little Elf.

157. **Ella:** Origin: English; Meaning: Other; Famous Namesake: Ella Fitzgerald

158. **Ellie:** Origin: French; Meaning: Bright Shining One

159. **Eloise:** Origin: English; Meaning: Healthy; Variation: Elouise

160. **Elsa:** Origin: Spanish; Meaning: Truth; Famous Namesake: Queen Elsa from *Frozen*

161. **Emily:** Origin: English; Meaning: Rival; Famous Namesake: Emily Dickinson

162. **Emma:** Origin: German; Meaning: Whole or Universal; Variation: Ima

163. **Emmy:** Origin: French; Meaning: Hardworking; Good for fans of the small screen – after all, there is no greater honor than an Emmy.

164. **Endora:** Origin: Greek; Meaning: Light

165. **Enid:** Origin: Welsh; Meaning: Soul or Life

166. **Esme:** Origin: French; Meaning: Esteemed or Loved Variation: Esmee

167. **Esther:** Origin: Persian; Meaning: Star; Variation: Ester
168. **Eva:** Origin: Latin; Meaning: Life or Living One; Variation: Ava
169. **Eve:** Origin: Biblical; Meaning: To Breathe or To Live; Variation: Evie
170. **Faith:** Origin: English; Meaning: To Trust; Variations: Fay, Fae, Faye
171. **Fancy:** Origin: English; Meaning: Like, Love, Inclination or Ornamental; Good for the pup you plan on always providing the finer things in life for.
172. **Fanny:** Origin: English; Meaning: Free; Variation: Fanni
173. **Feather:** Origin: English; Meaning: Bird Covering
174. **Felicity:** Origin: English; Meaning: Happiness; Good for fans of the 1990's show *Felicity*.
175. **FiFi:** Origin: French; Meaning: Addition to the Family
176. **Finley:** Origin: Irish; Meaning: Fair Hero; Variation: Finlay
177. **Fiona:** Origin: Scottish; Meaning: Fair; Famous Namesake: Princess Fiona from the *Shrek* movies.
178. **Firefly:** A fun name for your pup who is always flitting around the house.
179. **Fluffy:** Is your new girl a fluffy ball of fur? If the name fits, use it.
180. **Foxy:** Another name derived from the animal kingdom, Foxy could be perfect for your sly and mischievous pup.
181. **Franciacorta:** If you know your wine, you already know where the name Franciacorta comes from. Now, you just have to decide if this is a drink worthy of honoring your favorite new girl with.
182. **Francisca:** Origin: Spanish; Meaning: Free; Variation: Francis; Nickname: Frankie
183. **Frannie:** Origin: French; Meaning: Free One
184. **Frida:** Origin: German; Meaning: Peace; Variation: Frieda
185. **Fuzzy:** Does your pup have a shock of hair that seems impossible to control? If so, Fuzzy may be the perfect name to anoint her with.

186. **Gabby:** Origin: Hebrew; Meaning: God is My Strong Man; Variations: Gabriel, Gabrielle

187. **Geneva:** Origin: City in Switzerland; Meaning: Tribe Woman; Variation: Genevieve

188. **Georgia:** Origin: English; Meaning: Farmer or Earthworker; Variation: Georgiana; Famous Namesake: Georgia O'Keeffe

189. **Gertrude:** Origin: German; Meaning: Spear of Strength; Variation: Gertraud; Famous Namesake: Gertrude Stein

190. **Gidget:** Origin: English; Meaning: Combination of Girl and Midget; Famous Namesake: The Main Character from 1957 Novel *Gidget, The Little Girl with Big Ideas;* Good for small breed dogs.

191. **Gigi:** Origin: French; Meaning: Maid; Variation: Virginia

192. **Ginger:** Origin: English; Meaning: Reddish-Brown Spice; Good for your auburn colored pup.

193. **Ginny:** Origin: Latin; Meaning: Of the Virgin

194. **Gizmo:** This can be a cute name for your little pup who always seems to be into everything.

195. **Goldie:** Origin: English; Meaning: Gold

196. **Goldilocks:** From the children's classic, *Goldilocks and the Three Bears*, this is the perfect name for your inquisitive pup with light coloring.

197. **Gracie:** Origin: Latin; Meaning: God's Favor; Variations: Grace, Gracelyn; Famous Namesake: Grace Kelly

198. **Greta:** Origin: Swedish; Meaning: Pearl; Variation: Margareta; Famous Namesake: Greta Garbo

199. **Gypsy:** Does your pup seem like a wanderer? Then Gypsy may be just the name for her.

200. **Hannah:** Origin: Biblical; Meaning: Favor or Grace; Variation: Hanna

201. **Happy:** This is a name that says it all. If your pup is always full of pep and joy, then Happy could be quite fitting.

202. **Harley:** Origin: English; Meaning: Hare Clearing

203. **Harlow:** Origin: English; Meaning: Rock or Army

204. **Harper:** Origin: English; Meaning: Minstrel; Famous Namesake: Author Harper Lee
205. **Hazel:** Origin: English; Meaning: Light Brown Color; Variation: Haze
206. **Heather:** Origin: English; Meaning: Pink and White Flowers
207. **Heidi:** Origin: German; Meaning: Noble; Variation: Adelheid
208. **Henie:** Origin: English; Meaning: Ruler of the Home; Nickname: Hen
209. **Hershey:** Sweet as kisses, your pup may be perfectly suited for a name like Hershey.
210. **Holly:** Origin: English; Meaning: Holly Plant
211. **Honey:** Origin: English; Meaning: Sweet; Variations: Honeybear, Honeybee
212. **Hope:** Origin: English; Meaning: One of the Three Christian Virtues
213. **Inca:** Origin: Scandinavian; Meaning: Abundance
214. **India:** Origin: Country Name; Meaning: Body of Trembling Water, River; Nickname: Dia
215. **Iona:** Origin: Welsh; Meaning: Legendary Royalty
216. **Iris:** Origin: Greek; Meaning: Rainbow
217. **Isabella:** Origin: Spanish; Meaning: Devoted to God; Variation: Isabelle; Nicknames: Bell, Bella, Izzy
218. **Isadora:** Origin: Greek; Meaning: Gift of Isis
219. **Isis:** Origin: Egyptian; Meaning: Mythical Goddess of Magic
220. **Ivy:** Origin: English; Meaning: Climbing Plant with Small Yellow Flowers
221. **Jace:** Origin: Greek; Meaning: Healing
222. **Jackie:** Origin: French; Meaning: God is Gracious; Variation: Jacqueline
223. **Jade:** Origin: English; Meaning: Precious Stone; Good for your pup with green eyes.
224. **Jamaica:** Origin: Country Name

225. **Jasmine:** Origin: English; Meaning: Flower Name; Variations: Jasmin, Jasmyn, Jazmin, Jazmine

226. **Java:** Love your coffee and your mocha colored pup? Then Java may be the perfect name to tie your two loves in one.

227. **Jazzy:** Origin: English; Meaning: Ode to Jazz; Good for pet owners who love the musical genre.

228. **Jelena:** Origin: Russian; Meaning: Deer Stag; Variation: Elena

229. **Jelly Bean:** If you love your sweets and your pup is on the smaller side, Jelly Bean may be the perfect name for her.

230. **Jemina:** Origin: Hebrew; Meaning: Listened To

231. **Jennifer:** Origin: English; Meaning: Fair One; Variations: Guinevere, Jenifer

232. **Jessie:** Origin: Scottish; Meaning: Wealthy; Variations: Jess, Jessica

233. **Jill:** Origin: English; Meaning: Young; Variations: Jilly, Gillian

234. **Jinx:** If you've got a sly sense of humor and you want to give your pup a spunky name, Jinx may be exactly what you're looking for.

235. **Jojo:** Want a fun name that rolls off the tongue when you call it? Consider Jojo for your new girl.

236. **Josie:** Origin: English; Meaning: May God Add to the Family; Variation: Josephine

237. **Joy:** Origin: English; Meaning: Rejoicing; Variations: Joi, Joye

238. **Judy:** Origin: Biblical; Meaning: The Praised One. Also a good name if you like Judy Garland

239. **Julianna:** Origin: Latin; Meaning: Young; Variations: Juliana, Julianne

240. **Juliet:** Origin: English; Meaning: Youthful; Famous Namesake: Shakespeare's Juliet

241. **June:** Origin: English; Meaning: Sixth Month of the Year; Variation: June Bug

242. **Juno:** Origin: Roman Mythology; Meaning: Protector of Women and Marriage

243. **Justine:** Origin: French; Meaning: Upright; Variation: Justina
244. **Kahlua:** Origin: Spanish; Meaning: House of the Acolhua People; This is a coffee-vanilla flavored liquor that could be a fun name for your pup with mocha fur and a zany personality.
245. **Kaia:** Origin: Hawaiian; Meaning: The Sea
246. **Katie:** Origin: English; Meaning: Pure; Variations: Kate, Katherine
247. **Kayla:** Origin: English; Meaning: Keeper of the Keys; Variations: Kay, Kaley
248. **Kelsey:** Origin: English; Meaning: Fierce; Variations: Kelcey, Kelsi, Kelsie
249. **Kenya:** Remember those little Kewpie Dolls from your childhood? Well, if your pup is half as precious as they were (and of course she is.) then this could be just the name you were looking for.
250. **Kiki:** Origin: French; Meaning: Energy and Sparkle
251. **Kim:** Origin: English; Meaning: Noble or Brave; Variations: Kimberlee, Kimberleigh, Kimmie, Kimmy, Kym
252. **Kit:** Origin: Greek; Meaning: Carrier of Christ
253. **Kit Kat:** If your favorite sweet treat is a chocolate covered wafer, then perhaps your pup would benefit from this cute name that is oh so fun to say.
254. **Kira:** Origin: Russian; Meaning: Light; Nickname: Kir
255. **Kiwi:** Origin: New Zealand; Meaning: A Flightless Bird and a Tasty Fruit
256. **Koda:** This is simply a cute name to anoint your snuggly pup with.
257. **Kona:** Origin: Hawaiian; Meaning: Lady
258. **Lacey:** Origin: Irish; Meaning: From Lassy; Variations: Lacy, Laci
259. **Lady:** If you grew up watching Lady and the Tramp, you already know this can be a perfect name for your little love.

260. **Ladybug:** There is something special about ladybugs. In fact, some would say they bring good look. And there is no arguing that your new pup makes you feel quite lucky and loved. So maybe a bug name is exactly the way to go.

261. **Laika:** Origin: Russian; Meaning: Barker

262. **Lambchop:** Not all names have to have a special meaning. Sometimes, when it comes to naming your puppy, you just want a cute name that is fun to say. And Lambchop is certainly that.

263. **Lassie:** Origin: English; Meaning: Girl; Famous Namesake: None other than *the* Lassie – one of the most famous dogs there is.

264. **Leila:** Origin: Persian; Meaning: Dark Beauty; Variations: Layla, Laila, Leyla

265. **Lemon:** Origin: English; Meaning: Dear or Beloved

266. **Lena:** Origin: Scandinavian; Meaning: Torch; Famous Namesake: Lena Dunham

267. **Lexi:** Origin: Greek; Meaning: Defender of Man; Variation: Alexandra

268. **Libby:** Origin: Hebrew; Meaning: God is my Oath

269. **Liesel:** Origin: Dutch; Meaning: Pledged to God

270. **Lila:** Origin: English; Meaning: Of the People; Variation: Lyla

271. **Lily:** Origin: English; Meaning: Purity and Beauty; Variations: Lillie, Lilly

272. **Lindsay:** Origin: Scottish; Meaning: From the Island of the Lime Tree; Variations: Lindsey, Lindsie, Linzey

273. **Lizzie:** Origin: Hebrew; Meaning: God is Satisfaction; Variation: Lizzy

274. **Lois:** Origin: Greek; Meaning: More Desirable

275. **Lola:** Origin: Spanish; Meaning: Sorrow

276. **Lolita:** Origin: Spanish; Meaning: Lady of Sorrows

277. **Lollipop:** Just think, you could call her "Lolli" for short.

278. **Lolo:** Origin: English; Variation: Lo

279. **Loretta:** Origin: Italian; Meaning: Pure

280. **Love:** Your new pup is obviously your little love already, so maybe you could give her a name fitting of those feelings she inspires.

281. **Lucky:** We could all use a lucky charm, and your newest addition may just be that for you. Name her Lucky and you could seal the deal.

282. **Lucy:** Origin: Latin; Meaning: Born at Daylight; Variations: Luci, Lucie; Famous Namesake: Lucy Lu

283. **Lulu:** Origin: English; Meaning: Famous in War

284. **Luna:** Origin: Latin; Meaning: The Moon

285. **Lyric:** Origin: Greek; Meaning: Songlike

286. **Mabel:** Origin: Latin; Meaning: Beautiful and Lovable; Variations: Mabelle, Maybelle

287. **Mackenzie:** Origin: Scottish; Meaning: Favored One; Variations: Makenzie, Mckenzie; Nickname: Mac

288. **Macy:** Origin: French; Meaning: Weapon; Variations: Macie, Macey, Maci

289. **Madden:** Origin: Irish; Meaning: Little Dog

290. **Maddie:** Origin: French; Meaning: Woman from Magdala; Variation: Maddison

291. **Madonna:** Origin: Italian; Meaning: My Lady; Famous Namesake: Singer Madonna

292. **Magdalena:** Origin: Czechoslovakian; Meaning: Woman from Magdala; Variation: Magdalene

293. **Maggie:** Origin: Greek; Meaning: Pearl; Variations: Margery, Margaret

294. **Mai Tai:** This is a great drink for a fun and exciting night on the town, and it could be the perfect name for your energetic pup who is always looking to party.

295. **Maisie:** Origin: Persian; Meaning: Child of Light; Variation: Maisy

296. **Magic:** Perhaps you feel as though your pup has brought a bit of love and magic into your life. Give her a mystical name fitting of the transformation she has already influenced in your world.

297. **Mamie:** Origin: English; Meaning: Wished for Child

298. **Mandy:** Origin: English; Meaning: Lovable, Worthy of Love; Variation: Mandi
299. **Marigold:** Origin: English; Meaning: Golden Flower
300. **Marilyn:** Origin: English; Meaning: Rebellion; Variation: Famous Namesake: Marilyn Monroe
301. **Marley:** Origin: English; Meaning: March Meadow; Variation: Marly
302. **Marmalade:** Origin: Portuguese; Meaning: Preserves Made With Fruit Other Than Citrus
303. **Marshmallow:** Just the name for your sweet, ivory girl.
304. **Martha:** Origin: Aramaic; Meaning: Lady or Mistress; Variation: Marta
305. **Mary:** Origin: Biblical; Meaning: Wishing for Child; Variations: Maria, Marie, Maree; Famous Namesake: Mary Shelley, author of *Frankenstein*
306. **Mavi:** Origin: Turkish; Meaning: Blue; Variations: Mavee, Mavie, Mavy
307. **Maxine:** Origin: English; Meaning: The Greatest; Variation: Maxene
308. **May:** Origin: English; Meaning: Fifth Month or a Hawthorn Flower; Variation: Mae, Maya
309. **Meadow:** Origin: English; Meaning: From Nature; Famous Namesake: Tony Soprano's daughter on *The Soprano's*
310. **Meg:** Origin: Greek; Meaning: Pearl; Variations: Megan, Meggy
311. **Mellow:** Not every new puppy is spastic and all over the place. Some breeds are actually quite calm and cuddly. For those, Mellow might be the perfect name. Or, you could go for irony and name your erratic pup Mellow as well.
312. **Melody:** Origin: Greek; Meaning: Song or To Sing
313. **Mercedes:** Origin: Spanish; Meaning: Wages or Reward; Nickname: Dees
314. **Mercy:** Origin: Latin; Meaning: Goods or Wares, Also Merciful; Variation: Mercia
315. **Mia:** Origin: Italian; Meaning: My; Variations: Michal, Mya

316. **Midnight:** Do you have a pup with fur as black as night? If so, then midnight could be just the fitting name you are looking for.

317. **Milan:** Origin: Slavic; Meaning: Kind, Loving and Gracious; Variation: Milen

318. **Milene:** Origin: Russian; Meaning: People's Love; Nickname: Leeney

319. **Milly:** Origin: Latin; Meaning: Servant for the Temple, Free-Born, Noble; Variations: Millie, Miley

320. **Mimi:** Origin: English; Meaning: Resolute

321. **Minnie:** Origin: Dutch; Meaning: Desire and Protection; Variation: Wilhelmina

322. **Missy:** Origin: Greek; Meaning: Bee; Variation: Missie

323. **Misty:** Origin: English; Meaning: Foggy; Variation: Misti

324. **Mitzy:** Origin: Spanish; Meaning: Bitter, Rebellion; Variation: Mitsy

325. **Mocha:** Origin: Arabic; Meaning: Color and Coffee Name

326. **Molly:** Origin: English; Meaning: Wished For Child; Variation: Mollie

327. **Moon:** Frank Zappa was one of the first celebrities to give his daughter a unique name – Moon – and she has always claimed to love it. But this one might be more suited for a pup than a human baby.

328. **Mopsy:** This is another fun name that is more enjoyable to say than anything. Mopsy doesn't have any deeper meaning or origin, but that doesn't mean it still couldn't be the right name for your pup.

329. **Mouse:** For your pipsqueak pup, borrowing another animal name might be the way to go. Or in this case, a rodent – Mouse. This is another name that could also be a fun use of irony, if your pup is anything but small.

330. **Muffin:** Muffin is already a sweet pet-name used among lovers, so why not take advantage of it for the pet you love?

331. **Munchkin:** From the moment you held your new pup, she was already your little munchkin. Which is exactly why Munchkin may be just the name you're looking for.

332. **Myrtle:** Origin: English; Meaning: A Flowering Shrub; Variation: Myrtie

333. **Nadia:** Origin: Russian; Meaning: Hope; Variations: Nadya, Nadiya

334. **Nala:** Origin: Sanskrit; Meaning: Olive or Stem

335. **Nana:** Origin: Greek; Meaning: Grace, a Hawaiian Month

336. **Natalie:** Origin: Latin; Meaning: Christmas Day or Born at Christmas; Variations: Natalee, Natille; Great for your Christmas present pup.

337. **Nellie:** Origin: English; Meaning: Horn; Variation: Nell

338. **Nema:** Origin: Arabic; Meaning: Blessing or Thread

339. **Nessie:** Origin: Scottish; Meaning: Pure or Chaste; Famous Association: Nessie is often the nickname used for the Loch Ness Monster.

340. **Nikki:** Origin: French; Meaning: Victory of the People; Variation: Nicky

341. **Nina:** Origin: Russian; Meaning: Little Girl; Variation: Antonia

342. **Noodles:** Sure, Noodles isn't exactly a name with a deep or meaningful background. But maybe your pup is deserving of a fun name reminiscent of your favorite carb, but more important – a little silly and unique.

343. **Norma:** Origin: English; Meaning: Rule; Variation: Normina

344. **Nutmeg:** This tasty spice could serve as just what you've been looking for when it comes to naming your auburn pup.

345. **Octavia:** Origin: Ancient Roman; Meaning: Born Eighth; Nickname: Tavy

346. **Olive:** Origin: Latin; Meaning: Symbol of Peace; Nickname: Ollie

347. **Olivia:** Origin: Swedish; Meaning: Olive; Variations: Alivia, Olyvia, Liv, Livvy, Ollie

348. **Opal:** Origin: Sanskrit; Meaning: Jewel; Variation: Opaline

349. **Oreo:** What could possibly be a more fitting name for your black and white pup?

350. **Paisley** Origin: Latin; Meaning: Church or a Common Pattern

351. **Panda:** Another great name for your black and white puppy, Panda is a great way to use of another animals name as well. You could even call her Panda-Bear.

352. **Pandora:** Origin: Greek; Meaning: All Gifts; Fun Fact: Pandora was a mortal woman in Greek mythology who was given a gift from Zeus and told not to open it because it held all the troubles of the world. But her curiosity got the best of her and she opened it anyway, releasing all the ills we know today. A dark story, yes, but Pandora could still be a fitting name for your mischievous pup.

353. **Papillion:** Origin: French; Meaning: Butterfly; Nickname: Papi

354. **Paris:** Origin: Greek; Meaning: Son of Priam, also the Name of a City in France

355. **Patches:** Plenty of pups have really fun and unique patterns to their fur. If yours is adorned with patches, then perhaps Patches could be the perfect puppy name you've been looking for.

356. **Patsy:** Origin: Latin; Meaning: Regal or Noble; Variations: Pat, Patty

357. **Peaches:** Peaches are among the sweetest fruits, and the name is also a fun one to pass along. Can't you just hear yourself calling after your little Peaches already?

358. **Peanut:** Peanut, Peanut Butter, Nutty; they are all precious names for your little girl. Small breeds, especially, might be suited for the name Peanut.

359. **Pearl:** Origin: Latin; Meaning: Precious; Variations: Pearle, Pearlie, Perlie

360. **Pebbles:** Origin: English; Famous Namesake: Young Daughter on *The Flintstones.*

361. **Peek-a-Boo:** Go ahead, say it out loud. You can't do it without raising your voice an octave, can you? And that, is exactly why Peek-a-Boo makes a perfect puppy name. You can even call her Boo for short.

362. **Peep:** Do you have a little pipsqueak who is always yipping about? Then Peep might be the perfectly fitting name you've been searching for.

363. **Pee Wee:** Another great small breed name, Pee Wee is fun and reminiscent of childhood, while also being expertly suited for that tiny pup in your life.

364. **Penelope:** Origin: Greek; Meaning: White Shoulder of Duck; Nickname: Nelly

365. **Penny:** Origin: Greek; Meaning: Flower; Variation: Penni

366. **Pepper:** Do you have a darker pup, or maybe two puppies that could do with names fit for a pair? Either way, Pepper is a great puppy name – especially because you can call her Pep or Peppy for short. But don't be too quick to discount the possibility of a Salt and Pepper pair.

367. **Pepsi:** Another fitting name for a dark and bubbly pup is Pepsi. You could always call her Pepsi-Cola for fun.

368. **Petra** Origin: Greek; Meaning: Stone or Rock; Variation: Peta

369. **Petunia:** Origin: Native American; Meaning: Flower Name; Nickname: Tuney

370. **Phoebe:** Origin: Greek; Meaning: The Shining One, also a Greek Moon Goddess; Variation: Pheobe

371. **Pink:** This isn't a name that has to be reserved just for the singer. If you are a lover of all things pink yourself, why not share the name with your pup? You could also call her Pinky if it suits your tastes better.

372. **Pinot:** All lovers of wine know the enjoyment of a good Pinot. If that describes you, then giving your pup a wine name may be exactly the way to go.

373. **Piper:** Origin: English; Meaning: Someone who plays a flute.

374. **Pippa:** Origin: English; Meaning: Lover of Horses; Variation: Philippa; Famous Namesake: Pippa Middleton, sister of the Duchess of Cambridge.

375. **Pixie:** Origin: Swedish or Cornish; Meaning: Fairy; Variation: Pix

376. **Poet:** Maybe you have a way with words, or a deep appreciation for some of the world's best poets. If so, honoring that passion of yours by giving your pup a name like Poet could be the perfect way to go.

377. **Pokey:** The name Pokey can have so many meanings. It could be fitting for your inquisitive pup, or a fun throwback to doing the Hokey Pokey with your kids. One thing is for sure, this wouldn't be the best name for a person. But for a puppy? It could be perfect.

378. **Polly:** Origin: English; Meaning: Rebellion; Variation: Pollie

379. **Pom-Pom:** Is your new pup a sweet-as-can-be Pomeranian? If so, Pom Pom might be a great name to memorialize her personality and honor her breed.

380. **Pooch:** Sometimes there is hilarity in the obvious. Consider naming your pup Pooch if you want to show off your unique sense of humor when introducing her to others.

381. **Pookie:** This is one of those sweet pet names that actually makes a very sweet pet name as well. You know what we mean. Couples might refer to themselves as Pookie when expressing affection, which is exactly why it could also work well for the pup you love.

382. **Popcorn:** Do you have a pup who is always jumping around like popcorn leaping out of the air popper? If so, you already know this is the perfect name for her, right?

383. **Poppy:** Origin: Latin; Meaning: Flower; Variation: Pop

384. **Porkchop:** Much like Lambchop, this name serves to be silly and sweet at the same time. The good news is, you can usually find porkchop chew toys for your pup as well – a porkchop for your Porkchop.

385. **Possum:** Another name derived from the animal kingdom, Possum could be the perfect moniker for your skittish pup who is always more comfortable in your arms and away from strangers.

386. **Posy:** Origin: Greek; Meaning: Flower; Variations: Posey, Posie

387. **Precious:** Origin: Latin; Meaning: Price or Worth; Fun Fact: The novel *Push* and subsequent movie *Precious* popularized this name. However, with a darker plotline, you might not want to use that particular story as your inspiration for this name. Still, it is a sweet moniker all on its own.

388. **Primrose:** Origin: Latin; Meaning: First Rose; Variation: Nickname, Prim

389. **Princess:** Let's be honest: your new pup is already your princess. You love her, dote on her and have every intention of treating her just like royalty. Given that, calling her Princess makes perfect sense.

390. **Priscilla:** Origin: Roman; Meaning: Ancient; Variations: Prisca, Pris, Prissy

391. **Puddin:** Let's add this to the list of names that doesn't necessarily mean anything, but that sure is fun to say. Puddin also happens to be another popular pet name among couples, and we've already discovered those tend to work well for the pets we love.

392. **Puddles:** Do you live somewhere wet and rainy? The kind of locale where your pup is going to have the opportunity to jump around in puddles all the time? If so, you might as well embrace it now by giving her a name fitting of a puppy who is going to love getting wet and muddy.

393. **Pumpkin:** For your fall-born pup, Pumpkin could be just the name you're looking for. Plus, then you could always call her Pumpkin Pie as well.

394. **Punky:** This is just a fun name that might be fitting of your pups personality. Is she a bit mischievous and good at getting in trouble? Then Punky might actually be the name she's been waiting for all along.

395. **Puppy:** Sure, she won't always be a puppy – but that doesn't mean you can't have fun with this name meant to honor the sweet little pup she once was.

396. **Queenie:** Origin: English; Meaning: Woman, Royal Lady or Ruler; Variation: Queen

397. **Quinsy:** Origin: English; Meaning: Estate of the Fifth Son; Variation: Quinn

398. **Rainbow:** Maybe your pup marches to the beat of her own drum and has a uniqueness all her own – drawing attention to herself just like a rainbow. If that sounds about right, this could be the perfect name for her. Even better, you could call her Bow for short.

399. **Reba:** Origin: Biblical; Meaning: The Fourth, a Square; Variation: Rebecca

400. **Reese:** Origin: Welsh; Meaning: Arden or Fiery; Variations: Reece, Rees

401. **Rena:** Origin: Greek; Meaning: Reborn in French, Peaceful in Greek; Variations: Renee, Renita, Reenie, Renae

402. **Renata:** Origin: Italian; Meaning: Rebirth; Variation: Renate

403. **Riley:** Origin: English; Meaning: Courageous; Variations: Rylee, Ryleigh, Ryley, Rylie

404. **Ripley:** Origin: English; Meaning: From the Shouter's Meadow; Variation: Ripply

405. **Rosie:** Origin: English; Meaning: Flower Name; Variations: Rose, Rosebud, Rosy

406. **Roxanne:** Origin: Persian; Meaning: Dawn or Bright; Variations: Roxane, Roxy, Roxie

407. **Ruby:** Origin: English; Meaning: Jewel; Variation: Rubye

408. **Ruffles:** No greater meaning here, unless you have a deep love for Ruffles potato chips. But even without that – Ruffles is a fun name that could be perfectly suited for your sweet pup.

409. **Sabine:** Origin: French; Meaning: Ancient People in Central Italy; Variation: Sabina

410. **Sadie:** Origin: English; Meaning: Lady, Princess, Noblewoman; Variation: Sade

411. **Saffron:** Origin: English; Meaning: An Orange Spice

412. **Sage:** Origin: French; Meaning: Wise One; Variation: Sayge

413. **Sahara:** Yes, just like the desert. This could be the perfect name for your sandy colored pup.

414. **Sally:** Origin: Hebrew; Meaning: Princess; Or why not use the other spelling "Sallie"?

415. **Samantha:** Origin: English; Meaning: Listener; Variations: Sam, Sammy

416. **Sandy:** Origin: Greek; Meaning: Protector of Mankind; Variation: Sandra

417. **Sarah:** Origin: Hebrew; Meaning: Lady, Princess or Noblewoman; Variations: Sara, Suri

418. **Sasha:** Origin: Russian; Meaning: Defender of Man; Nickname: Sha

419. **Sassy:** This is a name that shouldn't need much explanation. Does your pup have a bit of an attitude? Does she think she's the one in charge? If you answered 'yes' to both of those questions, then Sassy might be the name she was born to have.

420. **Scampers:** Maybe your pup is prone to running off and scampering all over the place. If she loves to be on the run, Scampers might just be the perfect name for her.

421. **Scarlet:** Origin: English; Meaning: Red; Variation: Scarlett; Famous Namesake: Scarlett O'Hara from *Gone With the Wind*

422. **Scooter:** This is another great name for your pet who is always on the move. And you can even call her Scoot for short.

423. **Scout:** Origin: English; Meaning: One Who Gathers Information Covertly; Famous Namesake: Character in Harper Lee's *To Kill a Mockingbird*

424. **Shadow:** Origin: Shakespearean; Meaning: A Country Soldier; Variation: Shady

425. **Shasta:** A name that is fun to say and signifies an exuberant pup, do you think this could be the one you've been looking for?

426. **Silver:** Origin: English; Meaning: Precious Metal; Variation: Great for dogs with grey or silver coloring, like Weimaraners.

427. **Sissy:** Origin: English; Meaning: Blind; Variations: Cece, Celia, Cissy

428. **Skittles:** If this colorful candy is one of your favorites, it might be the perfect pick for your sweet pup.

429. **Skye:** Origin: English; Meaning: Sky; Variation: Sky

430. **Smidge:** If you've ever heard someone ask for "just a smidgen", you probably already know this is a word that refers to a small amount. So shortening it to Smidge could be fitting for your small pup, particularly if she is always going to remain teacup sized.

431. **Snarky:** Sarcastic, witty, snarky; they're all the same. And while your pup can't talk back, that doesn't mean you don't already know if this one would apply to her personality or not. Snarky might actually be the perfect fit.

432. **Snickers:** Perhaps Snickers Bars are your favorite candy. The great news is, the name also makes a great fit for the sweet pup in your life.

433. **Snookie:** So maybe this is a name of a silly reality television star, but that could be all the more reason to pass it on to you pup. After all, why not remain relevant and funny at the same time?

434. **Snowball:** This is a great name for your white, fluffy pup, particularly if she was born in the dead of winter.

435. **Snowflake:** Another one that fits your furry white pup to a 't'. And you could always call her Snow for short.

436. **Snuggles:** If your pup has already found her place in your lap, and is more likely to be resting there than anywhere else, Snuggles might be the name she was suited for all along.

437. **Sophie:** Origin: Greek; Meaning: Wisdom or Wise; Variations: Sophia, Sofie

438. **Sorbet:** This sweet treat actually translates really well into a puppy name. Try it out – call after your little Sorbet and see how it feels.

439. **Sparkle:** If you see your pup as being the light of your life, why not name her Sparkle and call it a day. It's a name fitting a diva, and one that is fun to say to boot.

440. **Spirit:** Maybe your girl has a strong and vibrant spirit you recognized from the first time you held her. If that's the case, naming her Spirit would make perfect sense.

441. **Sprinkles:** Everyone loves the sprinkles on top of a dessert, so why not give your pup this fun and lively name that could represent just how sweet she is.

442. **Squirt:** It's what you might have called your kid sister growing up – Squirt. But it turns out, this also makes a great name for the pup in your life as well.

443. **Star:** She's already the star of your life, so she might as well have the name to prove it.

444. **Steffi:** Origin: English; Meaning: Crowned in Victory; Variations: Steffy, Steffie, Stephanie

445. **Stella:** Origin: Latin; Meaning: Star; Nickname: Ella

446. **Storm:** Origin: English; Meaning: Tempest; Variation: Stormy

447. **Sugar Glider:** Have you ever seen a sugar glider? They are tiny little balls of fur with big eyes that just beg to be cuddled. Sound familiar? Giving your pup this name from the animal kingdom might just make perfect sense.

448. **Sunshine:** "You are my sunshine, my only sunshine." We've all heard the lyrics to the song. Do they apply to your little girl? If so, anointing her Sunshine might be the way to go.

449. **Sweet Pea:** This is another of those sweet pet names that can be perfectly suited for a puppy. Can't you just picture calling her Sweet Pea now?

450. **Sydney:** Origin: English; Meaning: Wide Island, South of the Water; Variation: Cydney

451. **Syrah:** Another great wine varietal, Syrah works as an ode to your favorite wine or just as a name standing all on its own.

452. **Taffy:** A sweet name for a sweet pup, you could also call her Laffy Taffy for fun.
453. **Talia:** Origin: Hebrew; Meaning: Dew of Heaven; Variations: Tahlia, Talya
454. **Tallulah:** Origin: Choctaw; Meaning: Leaping Waters; Nickname: Lulah
455. **Tanit:** Origin: Carthaginian Goddess; Worshipped in the ancient Mediterranean and North Africa; Equivalent to the Moon Goddess Astarte; Variations: Tanith, Tinnit, Tannou
456. **Tasha:** Origin: Russian; Meaning: Born at Christmas; Variation: Natasha
457. **Tayra:** Origin: Irish; Meaning: Elevated Place; Variations: Tarah, Tera, Terra
458. **Teegan:** Origin: English; Meaning: Good-Looking; Variations: Teagan, Taegan
459. **Tessa:** Origin: English; Meaning: Born Fourth; Variations: Tess, Theresa
460. **Tiara:** Origin: Greek; Meaning: Crown; Variation: Tyara
461. **Tickles:** This is a name kids, in particular, will get a kick out of. But admit it; you would smile every time you said it, as well.
462. **Tiffany:** Origin: Greek; Meaning: God Incarnate; Variations: Tiffani, Tiffiny; Famous Namesake: Tiffany's is a jewelry store in New York that has quite the reputation.
463. **Tiger:** Straight from the animal kingdom, this name could be the perfect fit for your ferocious little pup.
464. **Tinkerbell:** If you or your kids are fans of Peter Pan, honoring Pan's tiny flying friend with this name could be a big hit.
465. **Tizzy:** This is a fun name to say, without much of a deeper meaning. Still, it could be the perfect fit for your excitable pup.
466. **Tootsie:** Tootsie rolls are a sweet treat that have been around for ages, which makes them the perfect namesake for your sweet little girl.

467. **Tricky:** If your pup is playful and mischievous, then Tricky could be exactly the name you have been searching for.
468. **Trixie:** Origin: Latin; Meaning: Bringer of Joy; Variation: Trix
469. **Trudy:** Origin: German; Meaning: Universal Strength; Variation: Gertrude
470. **Tulip:** Origin: English; Meaning: Flower; Variation: Tulyp
471. **Valentina:** Origin: Italian; Meaning: Brave; Variations: Valentine, Tina
472. **Vanilla:** Origin: Spanish; Meaning: Little Pod; Nickname: Nilla
473. **Velvet:** Origin: English; Meaning: Soft
474. **Venezuela:** Do you have a love of travel, or a passion for Venezuela? Then this could be the perfect name for your girl. You might even want to call her Venla for short.
475. **Verona:** Origin: Italian; Meaning: City in Italy
476. **Violet:** Origin: Italian; Meaning: Purple Flower
477. **Volley:** This can be a fun name for any pup, but might be especially fitting if you have a love of volleyball yourself.
478. **Waffles:** We've already discovered that plenty of food names also make great puppy names, and Waffles only further proves this point. It sounds great at the dog park and could be the funny name that gets your kids laughing as well.
479. **Wendy:** Origin: English; Meaning: Family or Wanderer; Variations: Wenda, Wendi
480. **Whiskey:** It's a strong drink that is known to warm you up, so if your pup has already been warming your heart, Whiskey might be the perfect name for her.
481. **Whoopi:** Whoopi is a unique name with one famous namesake: Whoopi Goldberg. But whether you are hoping to memorialize the star or just like the name, there should be no doubt that it can be a fun moniker for your pup.
482. **Widget:** Plenty of puppy names are simply silly to say, and Widget is no exception. But it could still be the perfect name for your girl.

483. **Wiggles:** Puppies wiggle and scoot and move all over the place, so Wiggles just might be the uniquely suited name you've been looking for.

484. **Willa:** Origin: English; Meaning: Will or Desire; Variation: Willhemina

485. **Willow:** Origin: English; Meaning: Tree

486. **Wilma:** Origin: English; Meaning: Resolute Protector; Variation: Wylma

487. **Winnie:** Origin: English; Meaning: From a Friend's Town; Variations: Winifred, Winny

488. **Wrigley:** Just like the gum, Wrigley could fit perfectly for a puppy name.

489. **Xena:** Origin: Greek; Meaning: Welcoming or Hospitable; Variation: Xenia; Famous Namesake: Xena Warrior Princess

490. **Yasmine:** Origin: Persian; Meaning: Jasmine Flower; Variations: Jasmine, Yasmin

491. **Yoko:** Origin: Japanese; Meaning: Child; Variation: Youko; Famous Namesake: Yoko Ono

492. **Yumi:** This is a silly name that is just fun to say, but could be the perfect fit for your girl.

493. **Zailey:** This is a unique variation on Bailey that could be exactly the name you've been looking for.

494. **Zaria:** Origin: English (Modern); Meaning: City in Nigeria; Variation: Zahrah

495. **Zelda:** Origin: Yiddish; Meaning: Blessed or Happy; Variation: Griselda

496. **Zen:** You may not know this, but pets have been proven to help people relax and release stress. Which means that your new girl could be helping you to find your Zen. Maybe that makes Zen exactly the right name for her.

497. **Ziggy:** If you've ever sat back and watched your pup zig and zag all over the house, then Ziggy could be exactly the name you have been searching for.

498. **Zoey:** Origin: Greek; Meaning: Life; Variation: Zoe

499. **Zuni:** One last fun and silly name without much meaning. Zuni may not be a name you would find in the dictionary, but that doesn't mean it couldn't be perfectly suited for your girl.
500. **ZuZu:** This might seem like just another silly name, and on its surface, it is. But, if your new pup is a Shih Tzu – there may be no name more perfect then ZuZu.

Conclusion

I am so glad you joined us on the adventure of exploring all your puppy name options. By now, you have been introduced to well over 500 potential names throughout this book. Even if you don't pick one of the names mentioned in these pages, you have hopefully been inspired towards the name that is going to be the perfect fit for your sweet girl. A name you are going to love calling out for the next 10 to 15 years, and that she is going to love running towards every time she hears it.

Congratulations again on your latest addition. Having a puppy is going to change your life in so many ways, and she is going to bring you joy you likely didn't even know you were missing out on. The naming really is just the first step; you have a doggy lifetime of fun and memories ahead of you now.

The adventure is just beginning, and you still have so much excitement to come.

But I suppose that brings us to what comes next. Now that you have a name for your girl, what else do you need to know?

Don't worry, I've got you covered. I want to invite you to my website, where you will find a bonus chapter available to you as a reader of this book:

Titled: *Now That You've Got Your Name: 5 Things You Absolutely Must Know About Owning a New Puppy*, this bonus chapter is going to walk you through all the other important bits of information you will need as a new dog owner.

- Behaviors and Needs Vary By Breed
- All Dog Foods Are Not Created Equal
- Potty Training Takes Work
- Finding the Right Vet Matters
- Healthy Dogs Require Exercise

In addition, you can also download there a resource guide with useful dog training tools – "My Everyday Dog Training Tools – Free Resource Guide".

www.thedogtrainingplanet.com/bonus

Thank you so much for taking the time to read this book, and I sincerely hope that you have enjoyed it and that it has helped you.

Wishing you much love, joy and happiness with your newly named puppy.